W9-ABC-190

Happy Broken Crayons

an essay and tangent collection
about motherhood, life and
imperfection

by Katie Yackley Moore

This one is for the two greatest mothers a
girl could ever hope for

Terri Yackley and Angie Moore

I would need four more lifetimes
to thank you for all
that you have done for me.

Welcome Friends

I have a disclaimer for you: I have zero credentials to give advice to anyone about anything. I am a mess. I like to say a hot mess because it makes my constant tripping in this world seem a bit more alluring and exotic. But I still trip all the more, not limited to, but especially when I'm wearing heels.

This book is an anthology of some of the most significant seasons of my life. Having young children is such an amazing thing. It also can often feel like Groundhog Day. Caffeinate. Race. Rescue. Wipe. Clean. Cry. Cook. Hold. Sweat. Repeat. Repeat. Repeat. This is why the book is divided by seasons because if we sometimes don't stop to notice and breathe, it all goes by before we remember to exhale. Or laugh. Or enjoy it. It can all become so blurry, so fast.

This book is also meant to be a quick read: you can pick it up and read an excerpt in winter when you feel like you are getting buried alive in snow days, or you can read it cover to cover in all your spare time (ha ha ha ha). Again, I have no credentials, I am no expert, I am no doctor, I have no idea what I ate for breakfast today and I love a well placed swear word. If this serves as a guidebook to anything, I hope that it is a reminder that we are not alone. Motherhood can be an exhausting and isolating journey. And in this space of Instagram filters and gushing Facebook posts about how perfect and effortless every other parent appears to look (#blessed), it can feel like you are the only one who is not enjoying every freaking moment of raising humans. Please know this: you are not alone. Those people just aren't showing the hard. That is all. There isn't a filter that I found that is going to sugarcoat the reality of what it feels like to catch your child's vomit in your hands.

Being honest on the journey does not make you a bad parent. It makes you an honest one. You do not have to enjoy it all and more importantly, you do not need to pretend to be enjoying it all.

Real people are my absolute favorite. There is bravery in surfacing our struggles instead of swallowing them. Embracing our flawed lives and being connected in the cracks is infinitely more refreshing than hiding our true selves under masks of what society deems as perfect. I will take vulnerability served with a side of laughter any day. Pinterest served perfection no longer has a space at my table and I prefer it to be checked outside. Bring me your tears and failures and rock bottoms and I will hand you a beer without a glass and hold your hand and say without a hint of one upping, some of the most powerful words in our language: Me too. I know. I'm here. I'm here. I'm here.

I have a faded post-it note that is stuck to a wall in one of my favorite places: my closet. It is a quote that I stumbled upon long ago, "In the end, I am the only one who can give my children a happy mother that loves life."

I have read it countless times. I try to live by it, I really do. And I know often come up short. And I know that it is okay. And I know that the more honest and the more authentic that I live my life, the happier I am. And that is what I know my children will one day see.

So wherever you find yourself on this journey of life and parenthood, please join me in finding who you are. We get this one life. What if we tried, just as we have encouraged our own children's baby steps, to do a little bit every single day to take care of ourselves too, without apology? What if we just kept reaching for our own honest, authentic joy? What if that could be our legacy? What if we owned our glorious, chaotic happiness and decided to let go of the flawless image of what motherhood is supposed to appear to be? Cracked, spent, inappropriate, worn, loud, hopeful and stained, let's unite. You are my tribe.

Happy, broken and beautiful beings, thank you for coloring this world.

FALL

One day...

I will find the bottom of the laundry basket.
I will clean out my closet.
I will upload photos onto my computer.
I will order photos from said computer.
I will put those photos in an actual non-digital album.
I will buy complete sets of silverware.
I will own a tablecloth.
I will finish a thought.
I will finish a novel.
I will have a manicure that is free of glitter.
I will not have Disney songs stuck on replay in my mind.
I will eat food that is still warm.
I will carry a small purse.
I will not spend Saturdays on soccer fields.
I will read the whole Sunday paper.
I will have a house that will smell clean.
I will take a walk without looking for fairies.
I will not have anyone asking me questions about dinosaurs while
I'm driving.
I will remember where I left my tea.
I will walk across a room without stepping on a Lego.
I will not have cleats and princess shoes lining the entryway.
I will have windows that won't be smudged with small fingerprints.
I will take a shower uninterrupted.
I will only grab my keys when I walk out the door.
I will bake a cake from scratch.
I will be on time.

One day. All of that will happen in due time and that time won't
have anything on the days I spend with you. So for now, in this
moment, on this day, I am awake and present. I am yours. Let's have
a day that is anything but boring.

In Our Hands

I have been thinking a lot about children and bullying and school and the world and all that it is in our hands and all that is not. I have been thinking of the whirlwind of the mornings, of the making of sandwiches and the hair brushing and the do this and don't do that of it all that needs to happen to get out of the door with a hope of being on time. The things that we can control and the things that we can't. The people we love that fill our days and the people that drain our energies. How we react and how we let go. How there is not enough recess and far too much testing. Teachers who can't wait to retire and those that you hope never will.

Maybe we just need to kick this old school. Maybe we need to get back to the basics. Talk less, listen more. Less excuses, more showing up. Less getting bogged down in reality, more room for dreaming. Maybe it all starts younger than we think, the being there and the having fun. No rushing and wishing for them to be older even when it is so so hard.

I am not perfect. I think it is exhausting to even try to be. I mess up an endless number of times in a day. I am incapable of being punctual. I love wine. I check my phone more than any one person ever should. I wish we spent less time in the car and more time having dance parties. I wish I laughed more and nagged less. I long for more time with my kids and when I have more time, I sometimes feel overwhelmingly consumed by it all. In short, I am human. An honest one, but a bit of a hot mess all the while.

But on Friday I volunteered at my twins **preschool** and I remembered how beautiful it is to feel alive in a moment. A moment of play and imagination and joy and playdough and block building. How simple it truly can be and how much we can overcomplicate it. When I am there, present and awake with giggling four year olds, I can't help but to feel that no matter how many wrongs I have done, at least I've got this right.
Play. Build. Hold hands. Sing. Read. Paint. Listen. Laugh. Eat blueberries together. Repeat.

Children naturally absorb learning and acceptance. They may be young but they are old enough to love out loud. **Until we teach**

them differently, loving out loud is all that they know. They are the headlines of tomorrow. What the headline reads is all in our hands.

So maybe we just all need more of this:

And this:

I believe in this future.
Let's put our hands together on this one...

xoxo

To My Children on their First Day

This is what I want for you and wish for you. School is full of greatness but there are moments of stumbling that can happen throughout it. Your job is to be present and be a kid every day and leave any possible worrying for the grown-ups. That is what we are here for. We were given children to remember what joy feels like it. So my dear loves, here is your checklist for childhood living:

Try
Learn
Hope
Dream
Play
Laugh
Listen
Whisper
Read
Skip
Imagine
Create
Be kind
Be a kid
Be a student
Be a friend
Be you
One of a kind beautiful you

Be present and amazing things will follow. You try your best every day. And I promise I will try too. You have already made me proud. Let's do this loves...

To Lucy on Your 10th Birthday

Dearest Lucy...

Smart stunning girl. Ten years old today. Are you sure that's right? Yes, 10 it is. 10:24 pm on 10.2.04. Thank you for simplifying the math for me (we both know that it's not my strong suit).

So I've tried, cried and sweat more at home than at hot yoga to show you the good stuff over the last decade... I know I am no perfect teacher (*ahem:* nor are you the perfect student) but the world needs less attempts at perfection and more celebrations of our flaws. I do know time and time again that this what a child needs from their momma: to kiss your wounds when you fall, to be brave even when it is the last thing you feel like doing, to be kind no matter what. But what I haven't told you is that those things don't get any easier over time. You have to still be kind no matter what and be braver than what you think your small body can even hold. Because there are going to be more falls, inside and out, ones that will rock you to the core and I won't always be there to kiss each one. But keep going forward. You are resilience with a hefty side of potential. You've got this next decade by the horns. Please never doubt that.

Please know this: life is not fair. Your grandfather used to drive me insane by endlessly repeating that to me until it was my own mantra when I was old enough to realize that he was right. The world is not fair and it owes us nothing. We owe it with all the gifts entrusted in us to take it on each day and take it with a smile. Keep on smiling love and hold nothing back.

Don't forget this: you were born of tenacious spirit and mind. I would expect nothing less. Sugar and spice and everything nice? No thanks. I'll take my girls fierce, strong and all things mighty any day.

Always remember this: find your own happy and you will never feel at a loss for joy anywhere your life leads. Strive to be a better, more joyous you every day and let others worry about themselves. Don't get caught up in that type of worry of what everyone else thinks or has. Don't compare what they have to what you have. It will steal your joy. Nobody has time for that. The world needs more originals anyway.

Cheers to the next decade and embracing it loud and proud. Stay awake for the adventures ahead love. The world needs more eye openers and big dreamers.

The world needs you.

You are more than I could have ever hoped for. Happy birthday beauty.

Always...

Momma

How to Survive Back to School Shopping

I am a girl that loves summer. I love a break from the constant crazy of the school year. But I have four kids and somewhere around the 4th of July it strikes me that it would be amazing to complete a thought in the next few months. By the time the first week of August rolls in I get excited, borderline orgasmic, in seeing those glossy ads with shiny new Ninja Turtle notebooks on their covers. But what is the best way to shop for 26 glue sticks (true story) and about 800 other items while still keeping your kids happy and you sane? Of course you could go alone or do it online and if you can pull it off I commend you. Godspeed. But my "angels" love to pick out all of things for back to school. All. Of. The. Things. I can't really blame them. I used to love picking out things too as a kid but somehow I remember picking out a single Rainbow Brite pencil and one pink Trapper Keeper.

The times have changed and the lists have grown to beyond a Santa level long. Last year I left Office Depot in tears. *Actual stream down the face over the cost of dry erase marker tears.* Here is what I learned:

1. Go to Target. For three reasons: 1. They have everything you need. 2. They have everything you never realized how much you need. 3. Starbucks. 4. Palazzo pants. Okay that was four reasons. Math is hard. This is exactly why these kids need to go back to school.

2. Go early. Have you ever been to the back to school section of any store that prides itself in having a back to school section in the prime heat of an August day? It is one of the scariest sites you will ever see. It literally could be a bad scene from The Walking Dead. Zombies are clenching their school's token list, dressed in head to toe yoga wear wishing they were at yoga or anywhere else in the entire world mumbling about how many sharpened #2 pencils they need for their zombie children who are shouting that they *need* poly coated, one with prongs, four without, notebooks, the most expensive pencil pouch and that they have to go to the bathroom. Simultaneously. Go early. Get yourself some caffeine and smile, one of the only people there mumbling will be you.

3. Get yourself something happy. First. I made the mistake this August of looking in the grown up palazzo pant section last. Like a fool. We'd already been at Target for 4 hours; khaki clad employees were getting off their shifts that we rode the escalator in with. There wasn't one drop of patience left between the five of us for this grown up on trend pants smorgasbord. We had to abort. Never again will this rookie error occur. Live, learn, shop palazzo numero uno.

4. Give each older child their own list and basket. It's about time they started pulling their own weight. Cut up that giant list from hell into smaller lists of hell and let them have at it. It will be a scavenger hunt and the real winner will be you. It looks like someone will have 8 less composition books to seek out to and have more time to find the perfect 4" blunt end scissors for your first grader. Boom. Game changer.

5. Don't obsess over seeing the exact item cheaper somewhere else. This is a surefire way to want to take one of those freshly sharpened #2 pencils straight into your eyeball. That 5 cent glue stick at your local office store seems like the greatest bargain of all time until you get in there and realize they charge triple for all of the other shit you "need" and you've spent hours analyzing the cost of glue sticks instead of enjoying these last moments of summer. All equals out in the back to school retail wars. Go to a place that can reward you with a latte beforehand and have time for a cocktail poolside afterward.

Here's to a beautiful school year ahead and savoring the last taste of summer while it still within our grasp. And to the tireless teachers, I raise my glass to you. Thank you for always being more than we could hope for. I look at every item on that back to school list as one less thing that you have to purchase for your classroom. It is the very least we can do to begin to give back to you. Thank you is an understatement. In the future please feel free to include your favorite store to shop at (or your favorite cocktail) on those back to school lists so we can remember you throughout the year.

Here's to the survival…

And this was the result. Momma's going to need something stronger than caffeine.

And here are the things that I've come to learn with my four school age children that you really need to prepare for the school year.

1. **18,000 Sharpened No. 2 Pencils.** Hey kids, let's play a game called how many pencils will you be able to find at the end of the school year? Last June we had three if you count the one that was the same size as my pinkie. I feel like saying two and one eighth of a pencil would be a more mathematically accurate pencil count. We lost over 17,000 last year but somehow one prevailed and was sharpened to the point of being fit only for an American Girl doll. My children never cease to both amaze and confuse me.

2. **A New Lunchbox.** Please for the love of all things that make your nostrils burn, if your child's lunchbox is on its third or fourth year, you will smell your child before the bus doors open on the first day of school. In late July my 12-year-old realized that she packed a BANANA that she never ate on the last day of school. Sometimes you discover that there are bugs in your child's lunch that you never knew existed. Thanks science but we are starting this year fresh. You are welcome dear bus drivers.

3. **All of the Things that Come in Pouch Form.** I'm so sorry Mother Earth. I'm sure that these are not great for the planet but sometimes we just need convenience or we will never ever get out of the door. Ever. Juice pouch. Applesauce pouch. Yogurt pouch. Pouches I don't even know about yet. I want them ALL. Dear pouch inventors, keep on keeping on. I'm just going to put them up there with Google and Siri for my favorite parenting assistants (p.s. I love you).

4. **Thickened Skin.** Oh my lionesses, we must protect our cubs, yes. But we also need to help them thrive and grow, and we must know when to stay silent. There will be battles we fight for and battles that we need to let go. Reapply your thickened skin daily. And also know that it helps to bring treats to share to PTA meetings.

5. **Caffeine.** For you. For the teachers. For the bus drivers. For anyone over the age of 18 that is helping to keep our children safe and happy and reading on a daily basis. Make those lattes rain.

6. **ALL THE GLUE.** Oh do you think those 6 glue sticks are going to last the whole year? That's cute. Rookie, please. You get the Costco supreme 99 pack of glue sticks along with a Starbucks gift card for the teachers at the beginning of the year and EVERYONE WINS.

7. **A Clone.** I know. I'm just pipe dreaming over here. But that would be the greatest thing ever (aside from Amazon Prime and pouch formed food). A clone that could provide Uber services to all of the afterschool insanity and cook the 4:30 early bird special and the 8:30 post practice extra meal... now that could be life changing. This is why our kids need to stay in school to ensure that these things will happen.

8. **A Village.** If we can't have clones (get your head in the game Zuckerberg), this is the next best thing. I do not even know how I would survive without my village. They keep me sane, laughing and caffeinated. And we have each other's and our children's backs. It is a beautiful thing to have in parenthood and in life.

9. **A Gazillion Dollars.** Just for Target and Amazon alone. Kids are expensive. I'm pretty sure I would be a gazillionaire if I wasn't spending all my Benjamins on glue sticks. By Benjamins I mean my Redcard so I can save 5 percent (momma didn't raise no fool). Also note to self: invest in Elmer's stock.

10. **A Sense of Humor.** Life is wild and kids are hilarious so we might as well laugh together. Find your village and hug them hard. Seek the joy in the chaos. We all have moments of drowning and the connection is what can so often keep us afloat. Don't forget to take care of yourself and keep serving humor as a side dish to your goldfish and your wine pouches. We've got this.

Happy back to school everyone and thank you to our dear teachers, the unsung heroes among us. Godspeed... glue sticks, goldfish and gazillions.

You deserve it all.

My kids don't always sleep
in late but when they do it
comes with a 100% guarantee
that it is the first day of
school.

#awesome

Own It Sister

My four kids boarded the bus this morning. The first day of the last year at the same school. Fifth, third and first grade times two. Just. Like. That. I was thinking that the stars would align again in high school; that they would share the same halls again, maybe pass one another in the cafeteria, to have one another's backs and limbs and be the protectors of each other, just in case. But Lucy that too smart girl straightened me out like she usually does and told me that when the twins start high school that she will be in college. COLLEGE. Sweet mother of all things holy. Back it up time. I can't handle the mere thought of saving for college, let alone that she will one too soon of a day be leaving for it.

Today as I watched that bus pull away lugging my favorite cargo, loud, booming and stunning, my thoughts turned to motherhood. The bitter sweetness of it all. The being pulled in two directions like a marionette puppet of it all. The anchor of the roots, the releasing of the wings. The balancing act that somehow leaves you never feeling balanced. The dirty, clean, sick, healthy, arguing, giggling, late, sleepless, time too fast, time too slow, all-encompassing gravity of it all.

Motherhood has the ability to heal us and make us bleed. Sometimes all at once. Your sensations are more awake while the mind is more asleep. You have a superhero sixth sense about you that allows you to feel it all. Every. Thing. You absorb it all. Lightness and heaviness. Joy and heartache. Frustration, fierceness, closing and opening. It is all magnified.

And somehow we compare other mothers without thought. We judge like we have it all figured out. We judge like we are somehow perfect or our children are or that somehow that other mother is and *who does she think she is*. Like we've never had a rough day. Like we don't know what it feels like to be broken. Like we want to break someone else.

The new school year is an opportunity for a fresh start, not only for our children but for ourselves. How about we give each other a beautiful gift of judging one another less. We are all trying to keep our heads above the water and the last thing we need is more weight pulling us under. The idea that someone else has it easier, faster, skinnier, richer and all things better than you is a destructive game that is based on perception. It is a game that no one wins. I'd rather see women owning their strengths and their weaknesses and raising a glass to one another in all that makes us different and the celebration of what unites us. We are all part of the same tribe and how glorious it would be to see every woman flaunt it.

If you are crafty, own it.
If you are working outside of the home, own it.
If you are working inside of the home, own it.
If you haven't figured out this whole being an adult thing, own it.
If you are insanely proud of your child, own it.
If you are just trying to survive the day, own it.
If you go to yoga or just prefer to wear the pants, own it.
If you order pizza for the 3rd time this week or you make your own organic baby food, own it.

Natural births, epidurals, C-sections, adoptions, surrogates, we have all earned our battle scars. It is not a competition. Be. Who. You. Are. And protect each others backs and limbs like you would want your children to protect one another. The world needs more of that. It is not a slight thing to see the power that is a woman supporting another woman. We can be inspired by one another without tearing another one down. Let's retract the claws and unleash the fist pumps. We all deserve the accolades.

As for me, you can find me sometimes in heels, more often in yoga pants, working in and out of the home trying to make careers out of passions, all the while glowing in the shadows of this radiant crew that is growing up faster than my soul can catch up. I want to raise them in a world that builds instead of breaks.

Here's to owning it.

Always...

82. Just in case anyone was wondering how many stores you had to go to with your about to be in sixth grade daughter in search of the "perfect" backpack. And the winner?

The very first one at the very first store we looked at two months ago.

#middleschoolisgoingtobeablast

Instead of just
asking Sophia to change
her leggings with a small
hole in them,
I instead decided to
sharpie her leg.

#winning

9.11.01 The Aftermath of Compassion

Everyone remembers the shock of the world on September 11th. Where they were when the planes hit. The horror. The devastation. The glass. The smoke. The tears. Who they called to make sure they were okay. Who they weren't able to get a hold of. The bodies found. The bodies lost. The feeling of time standing still and forgetting to exhale.

I worked at The Washington Post and I have always felt that I was supposed to be there that day on the 16th floor at the interior of the nation's capital. I watched the smoke pour out onto the sky from the Pentagon. Rumors and tragic updates flew in and out like the waves of the ocean. The news couldn't be reported fast enough. When I left that day and went outside, the normally gridlocked streets were empty. DC was a ghost town. It felt like a deserted movie set. Eerily quiet. That is the point that I cried.

We remember the feel of that day. The places we listened to the news, the panic, loss and empathy. We remember the stories. The questions. The anger. The widows. The widowers. The missing. The darkness. The brave. And absolutely the heroes.

What we sometimes may forget is the aftermath of compassion. A nation that was shattered and found a way to see each other in a new light. A nation reunited. People called one another just to hear their voice. People called because time felt more fragile and more sacred. People cared. And people forgave. Strangers gave each other tissues on the street and told each other how deeply sorry they were. Acquaintances embraced one another. Parents held their children tighter. People helped in any way they possibly could. People listened with patience. People let go of what didn't matter and clutched closer to what did. We were one another's rocks. Kindness prevailed. Gentleness was savored. Love reigned.

From one of the most tragic of days came the most gracious humanity. A stunning aftermath that may have gotten slightly lost in the history books over the years. I hope we do even more than remember. I hope we keep that type of grace alive. I hope we listen again. Check in on one another again. Let's end conversations with love instead of anger. Let us treat people with the type of compassion that they deserve. Let us toast the joy of one another. It is time to pay hope forward.

In light, love and hope...

How NOT to be a MILF

**If you are my mom or my mother-in-law, it would be so lovely if you avoided reading this one. I think that you will enjoy this one called 9.11.01 The Aftermath of Compassion so much more. Thank you. You are the best.

How NOT to be a MILF

Ahhhh September. Fall is in the air. Kids are back to the classroom. Minivans are logging some serious miles and the back to school craziness is starting to feel a little less crazy. We have met all the teachers, gone to all the meetings, purchased enough Joe Corbi's to keep him in business for a long time and bought enough school supplies to stock an entire third world country. I now have 12 quality minutes a day to spend with my four kids that I'm not asking them to do their homework, change into their soccer cleats, practice the violin and not practice spinjitzu on their sister before I jam dinner into them at 4:30 so we can make a 5:00 practice that we will inevitably be late for. And then we return home at 8 so they can shower, have a snack (what the hell- did the early bird special not fill you up?), finish homework, read something before they are given a half ass rendition of "You are my sunshine" while being thrown into bed with the hopes that the stars have aligned and they brushed their own teeth without me asking them too. I'm sure that happened. I have barely enough energy to hook up with my husband and drink a glass of Merlot before I pass out on my husband who is already passed out.

So I get it. Life is wildly full. And we are so freaking tired. But I don't think we should give up on ourselves. All of the whirlwind of pick-ups and drop-offs lead to a number of mom-erations we will call them. You see the moms who really seem to have themselves together. Some are extraordinarily organized. Some are straight from a magazine stylish. Some are downright MILFs. And there are those of us who have had completely unfuckable, couldn't be more unattractive moments that if you put them together it could go into the best of "What Not to Wear's" highlight reel. I view motherhood as a sisterhood and feel that it is my calling to help a fellow sister get some. This is what I have learned over the last decade of motherhood about what *not* to do to become a MILF.

- **Mom Jeans**. Don't do it. If the button of your jeans is higher than your belly button than it is far too high. Only three people in the world can pull off the "on trend" high waisted look: Heidi Klum, Taylor Swift and Beyoncé. So unless you are 6 foot, 9 inches tall, weigh 98 pounds and blonde or have a child named Blue Ivy then please, please put the mom jeans down. Better yet, donate them to Goodwill. Halloween is coming and those jeans will go to a fun home that will put them to good comical use.

- **Too Many Stickers on the Back of Your Minivan.** I'm pretty positive that the number of stickers on your vehicle directly correlates to how frequently you have sex. As in the higher number of stickers that are there indicates the sex in your future is going to be less and less and less. That is so great that Presley made honor roll 17 times and Paisley plays lacrosse AND field hockey and that you love your German Shepherd. But in that long string of stick people wearing Mickey Mouse ears, I'm just going to take a gamble and say that the last time you had sex was when that small one at the end was conceived. And if you happen to be a man behind that Odyssey wheel, purchasing those stickers at Disneyworld, let's just say that you aren't exactly going to fall in the DILF category.

- **Christmas Sweaters.** Unless this is strictly for a laugh or an ugly Christmas sweater party, you might as well just wear a sign that says "I have given up on having sex again for the rest of my entire life." And if the sweater or vest or turtleneck lights up in any way, I strongly think that you consider joining a convent.

- **Debbie Downers.** At first I thought once you talked about what had you down that everything would be okay but now I realize that that is never going to happen. Your love of all things depressing, couldn't be any more of a buzzkill to be around. Time is valuable, don't waste it sucking the joy out of the room. Please get yourself some Cymbalta and a vibrator and then shoot me a message that you are ready to put the happy back in happy hour.

- **Non-stop Yoga Pant Wearers.** I am completely guilty of this, especially after having twins. Hell, I'm guilty of it right now while I type. I call it night to day wear. No need to change out of your pajamas to take your kids to the bus, or to pick them up, or change into a different pair of pajamas. By day 3, this gets to be downright disgusting. Your kids look at you with sympathy. Your spouse/partner is frightened. And you can't remember if you showered this week, not to mention the last time you actually went to yoga in your yoga pants. It is time to clean up, find something in your closet that makes you remember that you have a vagina and go somewhere with cloth tablecloths. You deserve it.

- **The Overachievers.** A little less Pinterest and a little more lingerie shopping is in order. You are so good and so into winning at so many things that I think we need to channel your energies into overachievement in the bedroom. Something tells me that someone was left high and dry last night because someone was up to the wee hours making an origami love note that looks like a swan and sushi made entirely out of kale and radishes (I'm sure both things won't end up in the school trash can). My kids will barely eat pizza so I just want to send you a gentle reminder that it is okay to choose to watch Real Housewives and drink straight tequila instead of spending endless hours over a chopping board.

And if you don't want to be a MILF, that is okay. But let's start with doing things that make us feel good about ourselves. Confidence is sexy and we shouldn't apologize for that. Being sexy radiates joy. People love happy people. People love to see confident, sexy, happy people naked. And there you have it- you are officially (or unofficially if you prefer) a MILF. And if it seems that right now you are too boggled in all of the day to day consumption of parenthood, just take it one step at a time. You will be a better mom for focusing on your own happiness once in a while.

Fake it until you own it. In more ways than one.

Cheers to the sisterhood of motherhood...

Own
it
sister.

What I Have Learned From My Kids First Week of School

This marks the first week ever that all four of my babes got on that big beautiful bus to head off to school. All day. All the live long lovely day. Seeing that bus was like spotting water in the desert. Is this only a mirage? Is this really truly happening?

Oh it happened. And it was glorious. It *is* glorious. You know how when you have toddlers and you run into mothers of school age children at Target and they say how fast the school day goes and they don't feel like they have much time at all and you're internally thinking, *"What the fuck is this bitch talking about? I don't think we should be friends anymore. I'm disinviting her to book club. But she does bring the good guacamole..."*

And you're smiling and nodding and pretending to relate when you only had six seconds of peace in your entire day and that occurred before your kids realized that you were in the bathroom. And you are on the verge of pouring your lukewarm latte on her freshly clean and blow dried hair that smells like coconut (*bitch!*) but you think better of it. Because you really need that latte.

But now I can sort of relate to it. Because the time that happens when you get a moment alone for the first time since the summer of 2004 is so fucking awesome that you just don't want it to end. You want to shout from the rooftops that you are naked! and alone! and it is the best day of your life! But then the neighbors might hear and ask you to watch their kids. Or ask you to put clothes on. So you retreat to your blog to let everyone know that instead. And the time does go by fast and before you even did a quarter of your to do list it is almost time for that bus to roll back up in your business. Damn.

I love my kids, I really do.

But to be given this time to feel and comprehend and breathe and create is borderline orgasmic. Just kidding. There is nothing borderline about it. IT IS FUCKING ORGASMIC.

I actually even this week developed this wild skin rash that was all red and itchy and hot to the touch. I really think it was a reaction to my mind freaking out because it has found its lost ability to process full thoughts again. MIND BLOWN. So it took it out on the skin because it knew that I would actually go see a doctor about that. Poor too often ignored mind, thanks for letting me know...

All is good now and healing and my mind is slowly acclimating to its new talents (i.e. thinking). I believe that some time alone should be required homework for all women (and men of course too but let's just vacation separately for now, okay?). It is a stunning form of therapy.

And yes there are to do lists and errands and real life and work projects but to choose when and how to do them, solely up to you, is where the therapy comes in. You feel that you can dictate the clock again for the first time in a long time.

So thank you, school days and brilliant patient teachers, you have given me, well... me. And there really aren't enough words to describe the gratitude in that.

My wish for
you:

Peace
Love
&
Hot Lattes

The Year of No

I have to say no to my children more times in a day that I care to admit. No cookies for breakfast. No flip flops at school. No cleats in the house. No TV before homework. No screaming while I'm screaming. No you can't have a puppy. Or an iguana. Or a playdate. No ninjas at the dinner table. No opening the packages I'm about to mail. Blast. You opened the packages I was about to mail. Timeout.

It is nos on top of nos around here. A no tower. All. Day. Long.

With children it feels like the nos are a necessity. Yes I prefer the yesses but it is the nos that give the structure of learning right from wrong. I give them in the (desperate) hope that my children will grow up to be happy, healthy adults that are able to function in society without their fingers in their noses and their shoes on the right feet. Or at least to not do the things that we did in our youth. For me the nos give them oxygen. Not the amount that makes them suffocate from too much restriction, or the other extreme that makes them take advantage and become spoiled. Just the beautiful between where they are able to breathe but they know that they are loved and that it matters how they behave as human beings.

But when it comes to adults it becomes a bit more blurry. We sometimes forget about our own oxygen that we so desperately need and deserve. We become yes machines. Yes to volunteering. Yes to all of the activities. Yes to making everything. Yes to the birthday parties. Yes to the field trips. Yes to all of the meetings. Yes to all of it. In the battle of super parents, I fold. I do not want to be super or parent in a way that exhausts me and stresses out my children. I'll take mediocre, thank you very much, with a giant side of sanity.

I am not dissing volunteering in anyway. In fact the world absolutely needs those willing to do extraordinarily selfless things for the pure benefit of knowing they have done something for the greater good of humanity. Our communities and schools are better places because of those willing to dedicate their precious time and energy into making them better. They are paid in thank yous and occasionally (but not often enough) in free food. I will absolutely give my hours to the non-profits that have personal meaning to me. I believe though, that if we say yes to every invitation, fundraiser, car wash, project, yard sale, cookie sale, playdate, meeting, potluck, campout, dance, instrument, sport, choir, theatre, festival, 5K run, class parent opening, coaching opportunity, troop leader position, "enrichment" activity and birthday bounce house party that it just might cloud what is truly important to us. If it is enough to make your head spin, just imagine what it could be doing to your child's.

My yes card is full.

So this year I am saying no. Unless something directly benefits the relationship that I have with my children or my close friendships, my career or my family, then it is quite simply not worth it. I am choosing them. I am choosing me. I am choosing the causes that we deeply care about. I will show them that we do give back, we just do it with intention. Why give our best selves to others and have little left to give at home? Our money and time are valuable things and it would do a world of good to invest them wisely.

Mother Teresa so eloquently said, "What can you do to promote world peace? Go home and love your family."

Cheers to that.

As I was curling first grader Sophia's hair before tonight's Daddy Daughter dance she said, "I look so different. People are going to think I'm a second grader."

#love

Advice for a Teenager I Adore

I can deny it all I want but the frightening fact is that one day my four children will be teenagers. Feisty, hopefully not wearing their pajamas to the mall, snarky 13-19 year olds. Everyone says enjoy the time when they are young because one day, not far from now, you will be pacing for your child to come home. I sometimes receive texts from my husband's cousin, a 14-year old seeking advice on every teenage issue imaginable. I appreciate that she confides in me and I hope that every teenager has an adult to be open with. I also feel grateful that I do not have to relive those years but it also makes me cringe at the thought that one soon day, I will be riding shot gun on the emotional roller coaster that will come from living in the same house as my future high school students (I know Mom, I know- those days will be payback time).

There is no denying that it is a different day and age then we, as parents, were growing up. My eight-year old knows how to do more on a computer than I did at the age of eighteen. There was no internet, cell phones or social media. Bullying was contained during school hours. It now has no boundaries. We, as adults, need to do our part to listen, advise and most importantly, be there. Here is the advice that I give to the teenagers that I adore now and will continue to give (with the hope that any single part of it is listened to):

- Stop scrolling incessantly.
- Pause on taking a selfie with your lips pursed.
- Take a social media breather.
- Put down your phone when someone is talking to you.
- Texting should not replace face-to-face conversations.
- Listen to your parents.
- Listen to your grandparents.
- You are loved by so many and more than you could ever realize.
- You are strong, smart and beautiful.
- Speak with respect.
- The internet is written in ink.
- Think before sending.
- Learn to say sorry, please and thank you.
- Forgive.
- Letting go is essential to your future happiness.

- Doing well in school is essential to your future.
- Saying no to what everyone else is doing is empowering.
- Think before piercing.
- Or tattooing.
- Use spellcheck.
- Learn from your mistakes.
- Dream big.
- Appreciate it all.
- Life is colorful. Try not to be beige.
- Perfection is overrated.
- Get a job.
- Do your chores.
- Ask how you can help.
- Dance.
- Happy people attract happy people.
- You can guess what negativity attracts.
- Try yoga.
- Try out for a team.
- Eat foods grown from the ground.
- Write in a journal.
- Read books that you love.
- You have permission to complain about something three times before creating a positive solution for it.
- Laugh with your friends.
- If someone is hurtful, they are not worth your time.
- Don't smoke.
- Wear your seatbelt.
- Learn to play an instrument.
- Have slumber parties.
- Volunteer.
- Recycle.
- Be grateful.
- Be you.
- Know that you are a miracle.
- Last but not at all least, hug your momma.

Here's
to
us.

The Type of Mom I Want to Be

I can picture her as clear as I can picture my mountain of laundry.

The type of mom I want to be.

She is patient.

So full of hope and awe and love that her skin radiates in the glow of it all.

She is not frazzled. Her voice doesn't raise. Her children... listen. They respect her. They want to do right by her. Her disappointment in them is the strongest punishment and once it is granted they wouldn't dare tempt their fate again.

She has time. She has time to play. On the floor. To put puzzles together. To put on Barbie's evening gown. To look at the clouds and the different shades of rocks that border the sidewalks path.

She is together. Hair washed, nails painted, clothes stylish. She doesn't lose herself in this journey of motherhood. She is there for her partner, a rock for her children, knows herself and keeps it all thriving, joyous and constant. She is so balanced and awake that you feel more alive in her presence.

She isn't weighed down by the endless domestic tasks of life. She just keeps going forward. She is so unburdened that she practically floats. The happiness of her family is her adventure and reward. She makes this world better. Without effort she is an artist, a coach, a dancer, a chef, a dreamer, a friend. Giver of time in an unrelenting circle to make this planet better than she found it.
She is all things beautiful.

I was her.

And then...

I had children. And then I had some more. I may still have pieces of this image of this mother but never actually all (or none) of these at the same time. I know what it feels like to have a baby that doesn't stop crying, a toddler that hangs from chandeliers, a preschooler that lets go of your hand in the street, a child with anxiety and what it feels like to be asked questions again and again and again. I haven't found the bottom of the laundry basket in a decade and I don't remember what it feels like to sleep uninterrupted through the night. Imperfection and survival are what I ~~excel at~~ try to excel at.

So I hold onto the hope of the ambition of this too-impossible-to-ever-be-real image of motherhood. I try to always end my days with gratitude. The gratitude of another day of being surrounded by all things beautiful and the reward of another day to embrace it all. Not to outdo the day before but to just soak it all in before my kids won't want to play with me on the floor anymore. Each day with young children is another chance to help your dreams and their reality collide in such a way that just might make this world better. At the very least, there will be laughter and that seems like a good place to start.

Cheers to you my friends... I think that you are all things beautiful.

You've
so
got
this
girl.

To My Daughter on her First Day of Middle School

Dearest Lucy,

I'm not sure how this day even got here. Somehow time has accelerated the older (and more fun) you have become and it seems like the opposite should be true. I'm in a bit of shock at the speed and ferocity of this whole motherhood experience.

I want you to know that I remember being eleven years old. I remember middle school. I remember how it feels to be on the cusp of not wanting to ever grow up and wanting more than anything to grow up. I remember feeling pulled in two opposite directions, often with the same force and desire, not wanting for change but yearning to grow. I remember the hard of it all.

Which is why you need to know that I believe in you. And I'm beyond proud of you. And I am in awe of your brave and kind soul. And that is what I need you to show up with every day from here on out: bravery and kindness. I know it sounds simple, but it's amazing how often the human race forgets one (or both) of those things each day and what a different place it would be if we didn't. There are people who may test your kindness and push the boundaries of your bravery. There are people who hurt and hurt others as if it is a game. There are people who think being cool or popular is somehow the greatest quality a person can obtain. There are people who may make you feel that you are somehow not enough.

If there is one promise I can make to you in this lifetime it is this: YOU ARE ENOUGH. Always have been. Always will be. You have been built to handle anything this world gives you, no matter how unfair or cruel or unsurmountable it may seem.

You can and will rise and prevail my love. Again and again. And you can do it with a smile. That is how your father and I made you and we will be relentless in our pursuit of watching you conquer life like the warrior that you are. *Just keep rising.*

We won't back down and we will never expect you to either.

You have intelligence, strength and fire and what you do with it is yours and yours alone. Don't dim or compromise your spark for anyone else. Ever. Boys are fun and great and all but they are only worth your time if they can see your worth. You, love, don't need to be like the rest of them. You be original, glorious you. Say yes to the things that bring you joy. Say no to the destructive. Put the blame on your parents. Do your chores. Work hard. Say please and thank you. Put the napkin in your lap. Be gracious. Be grateful. Be brave. Be kind. See beauty. See opportunity. See the light. Smile. And, above all else, keep on dancing.

You've so got this girl.

Here's to a new chapter in watching you rise.

Love you.
Always.
Momma

Today I volunteered at my children's elementary school book fair. It's always a sweet experience to see the kids pick out something new and shiny all on their own and watch their eyes light up when they hand you their money. All on their own.

But not every child brings money. Some forget. We are all human. We all forget things.

But some just don't have extra money for these things that in life that are, in fact, the extras.

It's hard to see those children that don't have enough for the extras watch those with enough buy something shiny and new.

The first grade teacher of my twins, a beautiful, gracious soul paid for not one, not two, but bought books for five different children in their class that didn't bring any money today. Everyone in her

class left with a bag to call
their own. Everyone left
smiling.

She didn't do it for gratitude
or accolades. But I want to give
her gratitude and accolades.

I think teachers are the
greatest people in the world.

To say you go above and beyond
is an understatement. You are
miracle workers...

#thankyou

Candy Coated Gratitude

I am a lucky one. I feel almost overwhelmed for that I have to be thankful for. Health, happiness, heat, amazing friends and family, chai tea, mojitos...

But you know what I'm feeling so blown away by, what makes my wine glass runneth over with glorious gratefulness? I know you are thinking my children and that seems cliché and of course, I have to say them or what am I, heartless? But that is only part of the equation.

It is that my children are fun.

This may be where you question that maybe I've been heartless in the past if I haven't fully appreciated that my children are fun. Doesn't everyone think that their children are fun? The thing is, I'm being completely honest here, for me, it has been a process to get here to the pure raw joy that they are and can be.

Some people reach their fun in pregnancy or are enamored with the baby stage. I loved being in the glow of that space in time but I never fully embraced that as my natural comfort zone. Toddlers can surely have fun moments but it is freaking exhausting keeping them from every dangerous situation that you never even realized before was dangerous. My twins as toddlers made many a friend reconsider whether or not they should go for a third child. For me, the candy coated part is childhood. And the ages that my kids are now- no longer toddlers, not yet teenagers, (overall) delicious.

There are still challenges, but there is a hell of a lot more laughter and I'll take that bliss any day. It doesn't feel like it is all about surviving moment to moment any more. It is about soaking in the happy. Fewer tantrums and timeouts and tears and they can dress themselves and want to be good friends to each other. The potential of the day feels so much more silver lined.

Right now, they are off of school and they are building Legos and making bracelets and I am writing. In another room. Yesterday I took them all bowling and it was actually fun. Seriously. The grocery store trip that followed was pushing it but still there is joy out there to be had in outings. Dreams can come true friends. This time of blissful parenthood before felt so foreign and far away that I just wasn't sure if it could ever really happen to me. And now that it is here like most things that are invaluable in life, I'm just trying to hold on to this ride for as long as I can. The days can be boundless but the years are fleeting.

Happy Thanksgiving and cheers to all that is small and mighty that you have to be thankful for...

Endless candy coated gratitude to you for reading.

Dear Halloween, Thanksgiving
and Christmas,

Thank you for making us last
longer than our assigned nine
months.

In gratitude,

Maternity Pants

The Other Place

I don't really know how it happened but one day I woke up and my children weren't babies. Or toddlers. They didn't need me to pour their cereal or lift them out of their crib. They didn't need me to dissolve pink syrup in the milk filled purple sippy cup. Sippy cups no longer live in our cabinets or more accurately, leaking on the stained fabric between faded car seats. The stroller in the trunk has long been replaced by lacrosse equipment. The sweet new baby smell has grown into the scent of sweat and the reminder to my nine year old that he needs to take a shower. Yes, right now.

Last weekend, they were all in the house, all doing their own thing. And it was quiet. Four kids. All independent. And *quiet*. My mind was blown. I asked my husband, "Is this really happening?" His response, "They're not yours anymore." My response, a hesitant bordering on the edge of tears, "Yes they are." *Who asked him anyway?* Shit.

They still need me. But it has evolved into the other place. I'm no longer in the thick of the everyday. Just. Like. That.

Before any of them rode a school bus, I used to take them to a toddler morning at a local roller skating rink where you could bring bikes and scooters and baby doll strollers and whatever you schlepped inside would instantly be no longer wanted by your child as soon as they saw the new big wheel that another child was riding. The whole thing was a hot mess but we NEEDED to get out of the house to be able to survive winter. The center of the rink was the thick of it. This is where there were seats for the nursing mommas, this where the full body tantrums happened, this is where the tears were relentless and the falls of the beginning skaters happened again and again. This is the place where everyone's hands were full. It was where mothers gave each other reassuring nods that they were not alone. They too, understood that you had to get out of the house no matter how difficult it was to leave and how challenging it was to make it through the present moment.

And then in the outer ring there would always be at least one momma on roller skates. She had older outer ring children that knew how to ride on skates or on bikes without training wheels.

They didn't need her hands any longer to hold them up. She still was there, but now more as an anchor than an appendage. Her hands were free. She was smiling. She earned the other place.

I never thought I'd be her.

But I am.

When you are caught in the thick of the tears at the roller rink or the grocery store meltdowns or the endless sleepless nights, it seems almost impossible that any other place exists. I am here to promise you this: one day you will be in your home and you will only hear the sounds of the outdoors. You will be able to complete a thought. You will be able to drink coffee while it is still hot. And it will scare the hell out of you. I also promise you this: it will be remarkable. You will have earned the time. You will have earned the quiet. You may even miss the noise. And it is okay if you don't.

And you are still needed. Every single day.

You are still the chef, the chauffeur, the laundry chief, the therapist, the mediator and the all-knowing master of whatever item your child loses or needs that day. You are still the queen bee.

For life.

And that outer ring has no end. It just keeps evolving to a different ring, a different place. Easier in so many ways, more challenging in others.

As much as it breaks us down, it builds us up. So whatever place you find yourself, please know that it is hard and it is beautiful and you will survive it. And somewhere there is a mother looking where you are and longs for just one day to have that place back. She misses with fervor the fullness that used to be in her hands. She misses the sound of it, the laughter in it, the smell of it, the wholeness and the hope of it all. And that is the heart wrenching bitter sweetness of all that being a mother is. It is an unparalleled journey.

Here's to all the places of motherhood. Here's to us.

You
are
enough.
You
are
more
than
enough.

Dear Younger Self,

I know that you think you know oh so many things already. And you do. And no one can ever take that away from you. But, I want you to remember that girl who was eight-years-old that you were in such a hurry to grow up from. I want you to remember what brought her joy; what made her laugh; what she dreamt about. That girl who wanted to only smile and skip and make the world greater. That girl who didn't get caught up in all the things that she was supposed to be or care about how liked she was. That girl who was unapologetic about being too much, too big, too small, too loud, too sensitive- she just kept skipping. I want you to carry a piece of her with you all of your days. Don't lose her. You are her.

In your life dear one, you are going to fall. In love, in life, in work, in pain. You are going to come to the cusp of losing it all. Again and again. You will have it all together. And you will crumble. You will be a walking contradiction. You will learn the real meaning of giving and taking. You will feel what it is like to have people chip away at the very soul of you without you even realizing it. You will be rejected. You will lose money. You will lose friends. You will think that you know people that you never really did. You will learn what it feels like to not be able to lift your head above the surface. You will grieve. Your voice will shake. Your eyes will look down for too long. You will disappoint yourself and the people you love. You will question everything. You will be physically and emotionally exhausted. You will find more tears within you than ever thought you would be capable of. You will know what it will feel like to be afraid at your core. You will know what it will feel like to both listen to and betray your own instincts. You will fail.

But here is the good news: it will all be okay. You will rise. Again and again. You will put on the heels and the lipstick and fake it until you own it. You will have people that will hold your hands and not want to leave your kitchen. Your friends will be your soulmates. You will know what it feels like to hold the weight of your own baby against your chest. You will watch your babies grow overnight. You will be the carrier of treasures and secrets and unwavering hope for your children. You will watch them take on fields and classrooms and stages and skip with wild abandon. You will see the most glorious work of your life through their eyes. You will know what it feels like to be chosen. You will chose them. You will chose you. You will find peace. You will let go. You will grow. You will find your fire. You will know resilience. You will know strength. You will fall back in love with the sound of your own laughter. You will be more courageous than you ever thought that you were capable of. You will live your life on your terms. You will be enough. Just as you are.

All will be okay.
You will love your life.
All of it (even 2016).
Promise.

WINTER

What NOT to Get My Kids this Holiday

It is upon us once again. The insane frenzy of all things bright, sparkly and overstimulating. The blinking commercials and overflowing catalogs have made my children want every toy ever made. Ever. This is where the parent filter needs to come into play. I am not trying to be a Scrooge but I am going to be honest here, Lorax style. I am the naked momma, I speak for all the (clothed) mommas who don't want their homes to turn into a Toys R Us.

The thing is, I love the holidays and the pure magic of watching it unfold through a child's eyes. But I like it simpler. I like the focus to be less on being a gluttonous consumer and more on the wonder of it all. And as for those toys that my kids "can't live without" (we will call that CLW here) that make both their first draft list and their final list? Let Santa bring them. Let's not steal Santa's thunder by giving them what's at the top of their list two days before Christmas. You know who are.

So here you go. Here is a brief list (I could probably think of oh so many more but I'm trying not to be a complete buzzkill) of what not to get my kids this holiday:

- **Anything with batteries.** Yeah that's right, I said it. I don't love loud, constant stimulation. Or baby dolls that seem possessed. Or ones that wet the bed (I'm pretty sure we have enough of that going around here anyway). I really don't even want to change the batteries on the shit that Santa brings from the CLW list. We have found that our kids attention spans with toys last much longer on toys that require a much more natural thing (drumroll please, I'm about to get serious): their imagination.

They really just want to eat pasta naked.

- **If it is sold via infomercial, it is probably going to suck in real life.** Unfortunately, we have lived and learned on this one.

- **Candy.** We are still working through last years heart shaped Valentine chocolates. You know who brings them Christmas candy? Santa baby. It is the ultimate stocking filler. Seriously, stop stealing his thunder. If anyone's giving my kids a sugar high it is going to be the guy who gets to live in the North Pole with Will Ferrell.

- **Would you want it in your home?** If the answer is remotely close to a hell no than please mother of all things holy, don't give (or regift) it to us.

- **Anything that breathes.** I can barely keep my children alive. If you give them a pet than you need to be prepared that it will be instantly regifted back to you.

- **Things that are completely too old for the recipient.** I'm looking at you Lego set of the Eiffel Tower. If you give my four year old something with over 250 pieces, please set aside the 17 hours it is going to take to help us put it together. Then stick around for the 44 seconds for it to be destructed. And then that bonus 17 hours again, please. Better yet, may I recommend a Lego gift card with a side of a vat of wine.

- **Things that are completely too young for the recipient.** I'm trying to not have them grow up too fast either. But if a toy is designed for the under 18 month generation, the above 18 month generation is going to see it as too babyish. You can even bet some smart 16 month olds aren't going to be feeling it either. I know it is the thought that counts, but for a toy that won't be played with, no matter how good of a deal it was PLEASE donate it to Toys for Tots or another fabulous non-profit instead.

The truth of it is that there are too many kids living without enough to give in excess to those who are lucky enough to already have plentiful gifts under their tree. Let's make sure that there is enough love to go around. Give back. Let's teach our kids to the same. A kinder more generous world could probably help bring the world peace that I'm really hoping finds its way to making more Santa CLW lists this year. Until then, please especially remember the no batteries request.

Wishing you all things merry...

What I Learned in Paradise

I have been back to reality for about a week and a half from having experienced one of the greatest trips of my life. Truthfully, I was in denial of reality until a few days ago when one of my children threw up all over the interior of our new car. That was just what I ~~needed~~ didn't realize I needed to remind myself to wake back up and remember that I wasn't in St. John any longer. If you have not been to St. John in the Virgin Islands, let me just tell you that it was probably the closest to paradise that I have ever been. Crystal blue waters, 85 degrees, stunning beaches, snorkeling, phenomenal food and the rum... I can't even begin to tell you how ridiculously enticing those rum drinks were. And did I mention that we didn't bring our kids?

Just my husband and I with another fabulous couple with a jeep and a villa. PARADISE. Leaving the door only required grabbing a map and a water bottle. If you have young children, I know that is really the part that sounds truly amazing. And it was.

I am not sure if I will get another chance in the next decade to escape real life again so I wanted to capture this moment in time, feeling that sun so close, and remembering that it actually happened; it wasn't just a dream though if I didn't have pictures and a fading tan line it would be hard for me to believe. Here is what I learned in paradise:

- **Silence is bliss.** Don't get me wrong. I love the energy and sounds of the world, especially those that come from my children. I try to not only embrace it, but to feed off of it and ignite me to play and have more fun in these days. But sometimes it is loud. Insanely high pitched screaming at all times loud. And I forget how therapeutic it can be still with my own mind. We don't realize how much noise fills our days until we have these rare stunning moments of quiet where we can just be aware of our own selves. I realized that this is why I crave yoga- that stillness and silence is priceless. On our trip, I would meditate on our deck and I could hear the sounds of tree frogs and nature and breath and peace and I fell in love with it all. Meditation could change this world.

- **The sun rejuvenates the spirit.** Vitamin D is our friend. There is so much talk about too much sun exposure, skin cancer, dark spots, certain hours that should be avoided in the day, and yadda yadda yadda that we have built up a certain fear of the sun. Some fear is healthy but too much that you avoid it and you are missing out on a beautiful, natural mood lifter and depression blocker. Let's throw on some sunscreen and go soak in some happiness.

- **Be present.** You know what you don't see in paradise (aside from anti-depressants)? People constantly checking their phones like their next breath depends on it. I would sometimes leave my phone in our room for an entire day and not even miss it. An entire day. I am back home and it is currently 7 inches away from me. But I'm instilling a parking lot policy for it when I'm with my kids. If we are outside than the phone is inside. I'm letting it charge when we play Go Fish. Being away helped me see how much more present and alive I can be when I'm giving my phone less power over me.

- **Be patient.** No worries, mon. Island time is a miraculous thing. Stress is non-existent. Slowing down is the nature of the lifestyle. It is hard to care how long you have to wait for your entrees to come when you have rum punch and sun kissed smiling people around you. Breathing in the moment and not being so pressed for every minute to go by faster than the next is what I hope to remember to take away. Every day. Slow down. Take it in. There is enough time for everything important in your life, you just have to be patient with yourself and awake in your life. Paradise is all around us, we just have to open our eyes to it. Booking a flight doesn't hurt either.

"Some people feel the rain. Others just get wet."
— Bob Marley

Until next time...

I believe selective memory is the key to happy parenting. Maybe I don't suck as much at this parenting thing as I think that I do and you know what? You don't either. Maybe it is having witnessed enough of your own childrens meltdowns and to see enough of other peoples to realize that we are not alone. The wildness of the child-raising experience connects us if we allow it to. The fact that it is fleeting reminds us to hold small hands while we can. It is not all cotton candy and cake pops with no repercussions; cavities will always emerge in one form or another.

But if we are honest and can tell the stories and laugh through the journey we will go through it smiling, or at the least, believing that we will make it.

We are going to be okay.

#selectivememoryforthewin

A Midwinters Day Meltdown

It often starts with a moment.

A moment in time where you wake up and think, *"What am I doing? Why am I here? Where am I going in life?"*

This for me happened of course at none other than Target.
The week before Christmas. At Target.
I had 12 minutes to make a return from an impulse Black Friday deal and buy 22 last minute items before I had to rush to pick my twins up from preschool to avoid being "that" mom. The late one. Again. Totally doable right?
I sped through the store like I was on a game show racing against the clock and about to win when I reached the checkout lane. Let me rephrase, I parked in a checkout lane. No movement. No eye contact. No one employee wanting to open another register for the 78 of us there looking frantically at the time on our cell phones.

I looked at the time on my cell phone. That can't be right. Let me look at my actual watch, it wouldn't lie to me. Oh no. I was Not. Going. To. Make. It.

Noooooooooooooo.

Say it isn't so. Tell me watch and cell phone time. Tell me you can make more time.

Then the tears came.

The thought of having to not only make a return trip to buy this (mostlyish) necessary random cart items but to have to bring my twins back with me to do it felt like a dagger to the soul. I checked my cart again to see if the tears were necessary or if I could abort and never return. *Damn it.* Among the stocking stuffers and teacher gifts were *toilet paper and caffeine.* Yes. A return trip was in order.

I waited in another too long line to ask in desperation if I could leave my cart with a promise to return, hopefully less sweaty but with two four year olds that may be among the world's most challenging people to shop with. We would be back. Please feel free to add tissues to the cart.

Deep breaths. Retrieved car from the garage along with everyone else doing the exact same thing at the exact same moment and only misidentified my car twice for two other black ones, one that actually didn't even resemble it.

Somewhere between my abandoned cart, my ridiculous to do list (is writing a note to remind myself to write a note to the kids in cursive from the freakin elf seriously on my to do list), inching along Christmas meets lunch hour insanity in Annapolis, I realized that I am a train wreck. And realized yet again that I AM NOT GOING TO MAKE IT.

Shit. I suck at being Santa. Maybe not Billy Bob Thornton in Bad Santa bad. But still Kris Kringle on Miracle on 34th Street, I am not. *Tears.*

It was time to phone a friend. By all things holy my friend Heidi said she would grab the twins for me from school. Her son is in their class and she has older twin boys. She told me she completely understood and to go turn around and save my cart. I love her.

I then cried at her generosity. WTF has happened to me? Get yourself together woman.

Deep breaths. I went back to that garage and acted like I owned it. I got this. Checked out with holiday joy in my voice. Headed to the liquor store with a spring in my step. Bought angelic friend Heidi a bottle of wine. And a case for our house (don't judge, it is the holiday season). Went and picked up my babes. And on that drive I woke up.

I realized it was me. I put the stress on me. A ridiculous unnecessary stress brought on by trying to overcomplicate my life. My kids only asked for a few things already purchased and my husband and I truly don't "need" anything (aside from the toilet paper and caffeine. And the case of wine). So why make it harder than it has to be?

I think that in my hopes to give my family this dreamy magical memorable holiday that I turn myself into June Cleaver's crazy twin. I can assure you that she is not at the top of anyone's Christmas list. What am I supposed to do? Not make enough cookies to fill a small bus? Not make our own hand sewn gifts when I don't even know how to sew? Not follow Martha's 12 nights of Christmas dinners all made from scratch that includes something called **mignonette gelee**?

Actually yes, that's exactly what I shouldn't do. And unless it brings you pure angel rejoicing joy, you probably shouldn't either. In our quest to create a "perfect" holiday we may actually lose all the traits of the type of person we want to actually spend the holiday with.

So please remind me of this if you seeing me crying in the dollar section next December. I want to be the girl you want to shop with. I want to be able to stand myself.

I know some people don't believe in resolutions but I personally feel that if the turn of the calendar motivates us to make positive changes in our lives than I am all for it. I love the idea of a fresh start, another chance to be who we aspire to be. So here are my hopes for this bright beautiful New Year and I would love for you to come along for the ride:

- Live more naked. More raw, honest, simple. Pare it all down. And then some more.
- Try not to be the cause of my own crazy.
- More yoga. Teach more. Take more. Make time for it and it will have a positive ripple effect on everything else in life.
- Write more. Blog more. Create more.
- Write a novel. That is my big scary get out of my own way goal and get out all of these words floating in my head that just need to be released onto paper already. I have had my soul set on this for too long for it not to come to life this year.
- Unplug more.
- Adore and appreciate more.
- Be present.
- Laugh, play, breathe.
- Repeat.

So here's to a year of embracing, living out loud and doing so stripped down, naked and honest to ourselves and each other.

Happy happy hopeful, imperfect new year to you...

"Don't pee on your sister's face."

Actual words I spoke tonight. Just in case you were wondering how this whole parenthood thing is going.

#killingit

Dear Momma Expecting Twins

I see you. I see you there with your "My Pod has Two Peas" shirt stretched to its capacity, gracefully unaware that there is a crescent moon of skin peering out from between where the shirt band and maternity pants band are supposed to meet. The look in your eyes is one of fear, joy and a touch of exhaustion, which my dear friend, is the perfect combination of twin preparation.

Five years ago I was where you are, wishing I had larger maternity shirts. I was terrified and excited and overwhelmed by it all. I don't know that any words can prepare you for the journey that you have a one way ticket on, but here are some things that I wish that I knew.

1. **It is hard.** So fucking hard. From the moment of conception my twins felt more challenging than my two other single children (or singletons but I've also thought that word was weird; more like a sitcom than a child description). I am not trying to scare you, I just want you to know that you are not alone when you feel like you can't quite get your head above water.

2. **It will get easier.** Keep on treading sister. There will come a day when you will know each baby's cry, which baby swing they each will prefer, make it through a day without tears (yours) and theirs (one day) and you will sleep for over 45 minutes at a time. It doesn't (typically) happen overnight but one day, I promise, it will.

3. **Fake it until you own it.** This will help you get to the easier point. Shower. Wear pants that have a zipper. Put on lip gloss. Shave something. Or go and have something waxed or painted without any children in tow. It will change your life. Take care of yourself even when it is the last thing you feel like doing. Especially when it is the last thing you feel like doing. Connecting to the pre-twin you will help connect you to the joy of the post-twin you.

4. **Marriage becomes more challenging.** Nothing tells someone that they are your soulmate when you punch them at 2 a.m. because you've been up all night with the babies on a continuous clock of teething torture. Stick it out loves and refer to #2. It will get easier. Help each other. Talk to each other. Appreciate each other. And

keep showing up. Gifts help. Flowers are good but pizza and not having to clean up the kitchen are fucking money.

5. Twins are double the joy and a gazillion times more mischief. Childproof. Now. The moment you see two heartbeats on the sonogram. Do it. But don't be surprised when they defy all these methods and still attempt to stick a screwdriver in an electrical outlet. By 15 months my twins were jumping out of cribs, breaking down pack and plays, raiding syrup from refrigerators, popping locks, starting heavy machinery and needed to have their diapers duct taped because, well, twins. And all of these things happened while I was 2 feet away. It is like living with a messy wild fugitive tiny monkey meets MacGyver. Times two. Wine helps. But keep the bottle on a ridiculously high shelf. Trust me.

6. **Take pictures.** Evidence helps backing up the things that happen in #5. One day, one far day from now, you will laugh. And toast yourself for surviving it.

7. **What you really need to register for: girlfriends, babysitters and wine.** These are the lifesavers and the unsung heroes that will help you get through it all. Line them up and never feel guilty for anything that helps you feel alive and happy and present. And if you have all three at the same time, embrace it and absorb it. Tell them thank you. But not in a note. Ain't nobody got time for that. Let go of the guilt of the thank you note. Just hug them and tell them and keep going forward love.

8. **You are a warrior.** Really you are. It is going to drive you insane that people are going to constantly come up to tell you how lucky you are (or the more insulting: how did *you* get so lucky) and you are going to be so tired that you can barely give them a half smile let alone grab them by the collar and scream "*What the hell are you talking about??*" You are just so damn tired and waiting, yearning for the easier point. The fun point. The point where you can acknowledge the being lucky. But the truth is you are. It is okay not to see or feel it all the time. It is okay to cry because you know that you are and you feel guilty for not being completely in love with it all. You are not alone. You have two human beings that are completely relying on you for their very survival and tears are more prevalent that laughter and you are leaking from every orifice in

your body and you miss your pre-maternity jeans and you weren't built with an extra arm and you want a better under eye concealer and a maid and no thank yous are spoken and no sleep is had and it is not a journey for the weak.

But you have been chosen, super woman. You were blessed in this life to bring two warriors into this world. It won't be easy but that doesn't mean that it won't be the most rewarding adventure that was entrusted to you. You are in charge of your greatness and theirs. There will be a moment that you could spill open with radiance because your life is so whole and you wouldn't want to change it for anything. Acknowledge the joy and hope of it all as each joyous and hopeful inch comes your way. And know that you are a rock star. You've got this. Own that cape baby.

Wishing you cheers, naps and all things hopeful...

Once someone asked me if
having twins was easy.

I laughed harder than I
have ever laughed in my
entire life.

For the Love of Winter

Winter is not exactly my favorite season. In fact, if we were to rank them, it wouldn't even be close. Winter would be the clear LOSER. And I don't think I'm alone.
According to my Facebook friends feed (and I have some serious kick ass friends) this is a rendition of how this past week of the snow vortex went down:

Day 1: WOOHOO KIDS!!! No School! We are sledding all day until we feel the need for puzzles, board games and reading every book on the shelf. Let me start on that gluten free coffee cake for breakfast. Get ready- this will be the Best. Day. Ever.

Day 2: Morning kids- no school. Again. Let's have some cereal bars, do some art and maybe this afternoon we could watch Finding Nemo. I might shake up today by adding a little espresso to my cocoa.

Day 3: Are you guys seriously still off? Ridiculous. Today we are watching bootlegged free movies online. All day. There may be some stale pop tarts somewhere. Please be a doll and hand momma that bottle of Bailey's to add to my cocoa.

Day 4: Let me just add some cocoa to my bottle of Bailey's.

Sound familiar? Since it is still (effin) January, I realized that we need to still weather a lot of this weather (pun unfortunately intended). I'm going to take a moment to look at the positives of winter (trust me, they are there, we just have to believe together). Our glass of Bailey's is half full around these parts. Or it's in need of a refill. Anyone want to pick up a case (or four) in their snowshoes?

Let's put on our parkas and do our best snow dance because here is what is to love about winter:

- **Think of it as working toward spring.** We have to date her, court her and work for her love. Winter is the foreplay that that seems like it will never end but with each passing day you know you are one step closer to the best orgasm ever that is spring. You have to earn your orgasms people.

- **Winter clothes are very forgiving.** Who cares how many holiday cookies you consume when your uniform for an entire 3 month period is oversized sweaters, leggings and boots? You know what is not forgiving? A bikini. Enough said.

- **Time to be productive indoors.** You know all of those projects that you never would dream of doing when it is nice outside (clean out the closets; reorganize the pantry; vacuum)? Now is the time to get er done. Or read more books. Or watch more movies. Do the things you love. Happiness is productive, complaining about the things we can't control is not.

- **Time to have sex by the fire.** No one wants to have sex by the fire in summer. That's just not even practical. But if your partner/significant other/friend with benefits lights a fire and you ~~shaved~~ possibly shaved your legs and you shed those sweaters and leggings... magic will happen. Winter can be very HOT. Like I said, it is time to be productive indoors.

- **Snow is beautiful.** I'm not being sassy here, it really is. There will always be a feeling of euphoria when the first flakes fall and to hear wide eyed children against glass panes whispering "snow"... and to see all of that brown and gray be covered in a blanket of pure white... magic. And I realize that there are a great number of people in this world that have never seen snow and may not ever get a chance to in their lifetimes. So maybe I shouldn't take it for granted. Maybe I should even embrace it.

Okay kids, let's get the sleds out. Though I am not going out without a giant thermos full of just for momma's special "cocoa."

Happy winter friends and just think that there only 54 days until spring...

Before kids, finding a trail of mud on the floor felt like the worst thing ever.

After kids, of all the possible trails they leave behind, mud is one of the best possible outcomes.

#goingtoneedmorefebreeze

The Top 3 Things You Should Say to a Mother

I am constantly ~~shocked~~ amazed by the questions and comments that come out of the mouths of complete strangers. Sometimes I wonder when I am out in public with my four children if there is a sign on me that reads "Please ask me anything at all. I have all the time in the world. The more personal the better. Please share how perfect your children were. I would *love* your advice."

I'm sure that it is with all good intentions, but sometimes there seems like there might not be a lot of filtering that happens when people speak to mothers. I'm sure the same is true for fathers but I'm also positive that if my husband was out solo with the four kids that people wouldn't be asking him "natural or in vitro?" or "C-section or vaginal?" so I'm aiming this for the ones with the uteruses. I want to help you well-meaning strangers who want to chat with our child towing selves. There are definitely wonderfully gracious things you can do and say to a mother that won't insult her but could possibly even make her day. And if you can't say something nice, please just walk away. Ignoring is always better than making a mother feel either ungrateful or that she's failing at this whole life.

So when you pass a mother who is out in the world with a child having a full body tantrum in the cereal aisle, here are three things that would be lovely for you to say to her (feel free to word them in your own personal way; kindness is the key):

- **You look great.** See how that sounds different from "you look tired." Mommas are not often complimented on their appearance, especially when they are out with their children. You saying that could quite possibly be the highlight of her day. Trust me.

- **Your children are beautiful.** Sometimes we need to remember that all children are miracles. And they are beautiful. This compliment will not only keep that in perspective for your benefit but help that overworked mom remember, "Oh yeah. They really *are* beautiful." It makes all of the crazy seem more manageable when we are reminded of the pure miracle of it all.

- **Can I help you with that?** Here is the scene: she has one kid hanging on the side of her cart, one sitting inside of it making Cheerios fly and one baby crying in her Bjorn and she's trying to heave a 52 count case of water anywhere it will fit in her overflowing cart so it won't crush the Cheerio thrower and you are inches away, eyes transfixed at the scene. If you have a moment take a deep breath and ask her if you can help her with that. She most likely is going to say "No thanks. I've got it." She secretly wants to be superwoman which is why she needs to buy so much water to stay hydrated. But she might just say yes and want to hug you for your generous offer. The point is that you offered. There is nothing slight about that.

I once had this angel of a woman approach me with the most patient eyes and asked me if she could follow me through the store and push one of my carts. (Yes- two carts. One to cart the children, one to cart the food = a walking ad for birth control). She said she had nowhere she needed to be and she was happy to offer a hand. Even though this was one of the most sincere and beautiful offers of help that I have ever received, I didn't take her up on it. I just couldn't put her through the four inevitable trips to the bathroom that were about to occur. But I don't forget that she offered. And that she saw past the crazy of it all and sensed that I could use a hand instead of judgement. Opening doors and offering assistance to strangers is a small way of showing the very large and happy idea that we have one another's back in this wild world. I hope that one day when I'm shopping alone that I, too, will channel my inner angel and help a sister out.
And maybe even give her a Starbucks gift card. That would really be the ultimate stranger gesture.

Let's pay it forward lovelies...

I was looking for the perfect meme to express how life has been lately.

But I couldn't really find one that showed a rock bottom with a trap door that you fall down head first into a thorn bush covered in poison ivy. That's pretty much where I'm at.

But on the bright side:

I had chocolate for dinner which I highly recommend.

We always have chocolate. Never forget.

#wineandchocolatecompleteme

I Get By With a Little Help...

I just don't even know what I would do without these glorious beings I call friends. They are everything I never knew how much I would need. I love that new friends emerge in the different phases of life. Though the faces may change, the dearest people to me all have a similar characteristic: the friendship is easy. The logistics might be at times challenging but the friendship at its core is natural. It is a beautiful thing and I am so grateful.

There are the ones that know everything there is to know about me and somehow still love me anyway. There are ones I see when far too much time has passed but somehow the conversation always picks up like it was never left. Some friends knew me before babies, some helped me survive pregnancies and there are the ones who know my children. There are the friends who know what it is like to really need to drink sangria. In the morning. Without judgement. And those I only see in classrooms and yoga studios. There are those that I can depend on to dance on a table with me and those that sense when I need to let go, release, cry and move forward. And to you dear friends that read this book, please know that I deeply adore you and read every comment, every e-mail, every message. I love to hear your words.

None of us are perfect. That would be completely irritating. Friends are human, beautifully so, and remind us that life is supposed to be fun. They are the reminders of how exceptionally marvelous it feels to laugh with your whole body involved. They are the ones that we cannot take for granted.

I do not know how I got so lucky. I need to start telling more people thank you. And I'm going to start right now. Thank you for the joy and the dedication. Thank you for the love. Thank you for saying to keep on going. Thank you for the tea. And definitely the wine. You are crazy fabulous, my friends.

Thank you for being.

Laughter with
girlfriends should be
the required homework of
motherhood.

#sisterhood

F#ck You Winter

Disclaimer: I am an eternal optimist. I see through rose colored glasses at a glass half full. I believe that everything will work out. Always.

But there comes a time every year when I stomp on those rose colored glasses and drop f-bombs out of my children's range of hearing. It happens around one of the last (sweet mother of all things holy it better be) snow storms of the season in March. MARCH.

Fuck. You. Winter.

I curse Mother Nature and her angry bitchy ways. My kids had a two day school week this week. The last time they went to school for 5 straight days was in the beginning of October. The weight of winter carries a burden that the heat of summer could never contend with. Winter feels stifling and heavy. Summer to me is all things open and free.

I don't live in New England or Chicago or Alaska or a land that is known for a crazy long ass snow filled winter; I don't know how those people do it (*seriously how do you do it?*). I live in Maryland, a state of mild lovely seasons that embraces warmth on the water; a drinking state with a boating problem. I want to hear a bird chirp and a flower emerge and feel that moment of unzipping your coat and breathing in the light of the sun without the bitchslap of a chill to your bones.

Today it is too cold to feel your face. Today your eyelids may freeze to your eyeballs. Today it is too cold for my husband's ATV to start so he can plow the driveway. He and my sons are old school shoveling it. It is actually orgasmic that he is outside and I am not. Thank you husband. I'm so glad I didn't stab you the other day when you asked what I did all day when all of the children were home on snow day #217.

So I've declared this day a day of gluttony and I will eat chocolate with a vengeance and drink Irish coffees like bikini season will never come. Who knows maybe it won't this year... fuck you endless dark stupid winter.

I've heard that you should wish for enough cold days so that you appreciate the warm ones. Done and done. Do you hear that Mother Nature? We surrender. You've granted us the winter wishes now we are ready for the spring ones. And we promise to be eternally grateful.

Until next winter.

Here's to embracing our Irish ways in the meantime…

Can't. Feel. Anything.

In the end,
I am the only one
that can give
my children
a happy mother
that loves life

(but sometimes I'm just
really really tired).

Top Ten Dreamy Life Resolutions

This is the year of talent, light and becoming unstuck. No more excuses or alibis. It is time for what and who is important and release the rest. A new start to living out loud. A year of saying no to the things that drain our energies and yes to those that ignite our strengths. It begins now.

Here are my top 10 life resolutions. Dreams really... let's just call them dreams. Ones that I believe I can make happen. The laundry and Pinterest are going to wait each day until I check off at least one (or several) of these babies. To me they are scary enough to push me into the wide awake life I yearn for yet attainable enough to reap the rewards. Now. Right now.

10. I will be present. My phone will no longer be an appendage.
9. I will let go. And slow down. And embrace. And write.
8. I will read more real actual books. And care less about not-so-real reality stars.
7. I will laugh. Until I snort.
6. I will show gratitude and grace and kindness. And own not just the type of mother I long to be but accept the one that I am.
5. I will love my home more than Target. And Anthropologie. Okay. Almost as much as I love Anthropologie.
4. I will listen and be more patient with my kids. Even when they're doing a 10 minute soliloquy about lunch boxes.
3. I will finish what I start. I will control time and will no longer give it permission to run over me with the force of a tractor trailer.
2. I will spend less time online and more time between the sheets.
1. I will take care of me.

Love, hope and strength to you...

Please remember this:

Broken Crayons Still Color

Stay Young, Superman

Mothers of boys let's unite. We need each other on this journey of ~~surviving~~ raising men.

It is absolutely true. Boys are a different breed.
Strong. Beautiful. Wild. Endearing. Unique habit to run instead of walk. Lovers of reptiles and mud. Drawn to engines. And playing basketball in the hallway.

To describe them as energetic is an understatement.

I have two boys that bring fire and balance to our house. One constructs. One deconstructs. Both imaginations run supreme. Give them a pirate sword and a bin of Legos and they will be effortlessly entertained. All day.

They are the jumpers of furniture, stealth ninjas on missions, secret spies, snowboarders, builders, mechanics, karate experts, the hiders and the seekers. And they are constant. There isn't much of a breather. I'm pretty sure that video games were first created by a mother with a desperation for her boys *to sit down for a second for goodness sake already*. Life is a whirlwind of hot wheels, monster trucks, fireman hats and mud laden cleats. On a carpet that might have been white in a former life.

But their spark is none other.

I am exhausted and in awe of it all at the same time.

My wish for them is to stay young a little longer. To wear superhero capes to the grocery store. To play outside indefinitely. To roll down hills that feel like mountains. To earn those grass stains. To tell knock knock jokes. To just keep building. To create big amazing things that don't yet exist. But should. To color outside the lines. To know when to listen. And when to speak up. To know that it is okay to love out loud. To embrace their emotions and bring them to the table. To say please, thank you, I'm sorry and excuse me. To hold the door open. And hug their Momma. To never stop imagining. Ever.

Boys will be men soon enough. Super boys are the only things we can use to create super men. So let's embrace it.

And it doesn't hurt to make sure that we have working smoke alarms.

Let's hear it for the boys...

Brothers. Now I am scared about what they are plotting.

Niko: Who made the first
elevator?

Micah: God. God made it.

Looks like that is one less
Google search that I have to
do.

#thanksmicah #andGod

What She Really Wants this Valentine's Day

Dear those who want to make someone happy this Valentine's Day,

I know, I know. It is a Hallmark holiday. Another commercial holiday to sell cards, roses and overpriced chocolates. The good news? She doesn't want that anyway. One surefire way to piss her off? Do nothing. Yes the holiday is ridiculous but that doesn't mean that the premise is. Love reigns baby. You show some love and you will be thanked. Tremendously.

By talking about love I don't mean romance though sometimes they can't help but to intertwine. I don't want to come across as cynical, but I find romance to be slightly nauseating. Unless you are Pablo Neruda, your poem might leave something to be desired. Leave the poems and red roses for *The Bachelor.*

There's a reason those relationships typically don't last longer than 3 ~~months~~ weeks. Romance can't touch the depth of being in love. Love trumps romance. Every. Time. I believe in a redefined love- a stronger, more genuine form of romance. So how do you make that love so steamy, sexy and smoking hot? Want to know what she truly desires this holiday (and every day that follows)? Stick with me and read the guide below. Good things will ~~cum~~ come to you love.

Here is how we can bring sexy back:

- **Vacuuming is foreplay**. Truly. Do it for her. Have fun doing it. Throw a little dance in there. You will get some.

- **Learning how to make rainbow looms is unbelievably attractive.** When you take time to spend time with whatever your kids are interested in it is a beautiful thing to witness. That will make the one you love ridiculously happy. Happiness brings reconnection. Reconnection brings nudity after your rainbow loomers are tucked in bed.

- **Not cooking and cleaning is the greatest. Ever.** I have yet to meet a woman who doesn't melt at the magic words, "Do you want to go out to dinner tonight?" I love to cook but after making 18 meals a day, every day for a decade, there are no sexier words that could be voiced. Everyone wants, desires and deserves a break sometimes. Think of what you could do with all of that bonus time not spent in the kitchen.

- **Eff chocolate, give wine.** No woman has ever felt sexy after housing an entire box of Russell Stovers. Keep filling her glass of Merlot, on the other hand, and her inner goddess will not be able to contain her gratitude.

- **Texts, cards and post it notes.** It doesn't matter as much which one you choose, so long as you choose one. Remind her in your own words how amazing she is, how hot she is and how grateful you are that she chose you. Never underestimate the value of gratitude and compliments. I am going to let you in on something huge: women need to feel valued. What you give her emotionally, will pay off for you physically. Words are free but all too often underused. There was something about her that made you want to have a second date- tell her why. She will feel grateful, loved and lucky. You will feel grateful, loved and get lucky. Simple equation baby.

You don't have to be Ryan Gosling to get your message across. I mean, it helps. But after your dinner out you can put post its up around the house telling her how much she rocks with a full vat of wine and The Notebook on in the background while you vacuum.

It will be a good night for you my friend.

So there you go. Women are not such hard creatures to understand after all.
You are welcome.

Movies can keep
the romance.

I'd rather have
the love.

10 Thoughts that I Had During my First Bikram Yoga Class

I may be a yoga instructor but Bikram still intimidates me. I have avoided it for far too long because something about that 104 degree room and the idea of the same 26 poses just didn't strike my Zen fancy. But then a Groupon came my way and I figured it was time to give heat a chance. When I walked into that stifling room for the first time I was intrigued, excited and scared shitless.

Here are ten thoughts that crossed and lingered too long on my mind during my first Bikram class:

1. **Is it too late to run out of this room?** Did I just walk into a sauna? Surely they just keep it this hot to welcome us. I've broken a sweat just in unrolling my mat. I'll just be sure to be in the back row in case I decide to go for a Starbucks run instead. Oh no. The instructor closed the door. Arrivederci Caramel Macchiato. It is okay. I've got this.

2. **Am I doing this right?** I don't got this. Excuse me... what is this breath work and why are we standing? I'm not following. I guess I'll just pretend that this is all normal and we all look completely normal. Note to self: do not try this breath in public. Ever.

3. **Sweet fancy Moses, her body is ridiculous.** Dear front and center girl, I see your better than J. Lo abs and your barely covering your cheeks spandex shorts. WE ALL SEE YOU. You are front and center posing like a gazelle in front of a wall full of mirrors. Bitch. I mean I know yoga isn't a competition but I cannot bring myself to stop staring at her. Wait is that J. Lo? I'm pretty sure it is. Or her more built body double. I'm going to need to watch Monster-in-Law later to confirm.

4. **I'm sweating more than anyone else in the history of ever.** ARE WE ON THE SUN RIGHT NOW? Is anyone else finding it damn near impossible to breathe? Has anyone else's mat turned into a slip n' slide? I'm so overdressed and I'm only wearing a tank top.

5. **Correction: the guy next to me is sweating more than anyone else in the history of ever.** I'm not trying to judge you yet I cannot

look away. If I'm attempting to balance on a slip n' slide than that guy is doing tree pose on top of Niagara Falls. Could we get Mr. Itty Bitty Spandex an extra towel? Or all of the towels? Maybe a mop? Rain barrel? If he's coming here to get laid than I am so sorry friend but it's not going to happen. Maybe you'll have better luck at Zumba.

6. **I should have done some training for this.** My body has never before been so pissed off at me. It's like deciding while eating a banana split to drop it to go complete a triathlon. Stupid fucking Groupon.

7. **I want to get a tattoo.** I am channeling all of my energies into fantasizing about being one of the almost-naked-I-have-Chinese-food-in-my-fridge-older-than-them-built-like-gladiators girls in the front row. They are barely even sweating. J. Lo and I shall become besties and drink wheatgrass after front and center Bikram together. And we will travel to Thailand and get small Om tattoos somewhere on our ab area so the wannabes in the back row will have to squint to read them. This class is the best thing ever.

8. **Is this class ever going to actually end?** Did I misread the description and sign up for a 900 minute class instead of a 90 minute one? Now all of my fantasies are about snow and Antarctica. Fuck Thailand. I'm sorry Thailand, nothing against you it's just I need to be among Eskimos right now. At least we've made our way on to the floor which is good because I'm not sure that I'll ever be able to stand again. I could have gone to Starbucks AND watched Monster-in-Law AND drank a margarita in this amount of time. I. AM. SO. THIRSTY.

9. **Thank you Mother of all things holy, the instructor dimmed the lights.** The end is near right?! Please tell me it is and don't you dare lie. I'll cut a bitch in spandex. I'm not scared. It is official, the end is near! The end is near! I was so kidding about the stabbing thing. I'm so happy. I want to embrace my spandex friends. I've never been more excited for darkness. Savasana you are the greatest thing that has ever happened to me.

10. **I survived.** I actually made it. Exhausted like how you would feel if you had your intestines ripped out of you, to be cleaned,

ironed, neatly folded and then put back in again while using no drugs, of course. And wow. I actually feel like a bad ass warrior. Sweaty, spent and glorious. That Savasana put it all into delicious perspective for me. God bless laying down. This. This is the feeling I guess we all strive for- overcoming our minds so that our bodies will thank us. This is detox at its natural crazy best. A celebration of what the body can do and a release of the things that need to be let go of. Bikram you have sold me though I may need to work on the abs a wee bit more before heading back.

I can't wait to shower (maybe one where I'm sitting down; I suppose that's called a bath but I don't want to swim in my current sweat situation). A sit shower it will be. And I'm actually sort of looking forward to the next class. I have no choice in it, really. Groupon's got me for 14 more.

Cheers and Namaste to you warriors...
May your hot yoga experience be paved with extra towels.

Doing snow angels naked in this is what
Bikram fantasies are made of.

There's nothing quite like
the morning alarm clock
that is your child coughing
directly into your mouth.

#goodmorningtoyoutoo

The Mirage of the Pretty Perfect Life

I have a confession. I have a love/don't love so much relationship with social media.

There is much to love about it: the connection and reconnection and the high school crushes and the puppies and babies and beaches and the really hilarious memes. There is also the joy of seeing and hearing life updates from the people that you adore, no matter how many miles or how much time has separated you. And my two careers of being a writer and a real estate agent actually greatly depend on me having a social media presence. I can honestly say that Facebook does help me feed my children and I am eternally grateful for that.

And it is free to join. Brilliant.

But here is the other side of social media: the mirage of the pretty, shiny, perfect life.

People that you know (or almost do or some not really at all) are out there drinking perfect lattes in perfect clean white blouses in perfect coffee shops in Switzerland, wearing the perfect shade of red lipstick while their perfect baby sleeps in a perfect pram. And you think of how deprived your babies are because not one of them ever had a pram. Or even really slept. But maybe if they had a pram they would have. And you couldn't even keep your wedding dress clean, let alone a white shirt that comes within five feet of any shade of lipstick. Momma please. I beg you, show me that latte spill just a little bit on that shirt. Or at least tell me what Instagram filter you are using. Is it Amaro? Valencia? #askingforafriend.

The other day I was caught in a Facebook life spiral where you lose track of all time and all sense of reality, and I was looking at a friend of a friend's cousin's honeymoon pictures in Bora Bora. And instead of thinking what am I doing, I don't even know these people, shut it down woman... this is what I thought: I AM A LOSER. I HAVE NEVER BEEN TO BORA BORA. I DON'T EVEN KNOW WHERE THAT IS. I'm terrible at geography. And math. Which is probably why I'm not in a different country right at this very moment like everyone else in my Facebook feed, doing amazing things in amazing places. Now I must go drown myself in Pinot Noir and salt and vinegar chips. But not before I see some more of these complete strangers wedding photos of their dog as a ring bearer.

I might be alone on this (especially maybe and hopefully on that last part) but I think that it would be refreshing if we posted a little less of the perfect and a little more of the real life. The hard, the struggles, the kid meltdowns at Target. Fewer filters, more honesty. Less perfect, shiny Christmas cards and more messages saying that this year has been on the harder side and I just can't pretend that it hasn't been so this holiday season I'm going to save some stamps and not mail cards but please know that I love you and I wish you all the happiness.

That's what I did last December. And that's most likely what I'm going to do this December. And if you've had a happy shiny year please know that I want to hear about that too. I want to celebrate your joy. I want to see your trips. I want to see you thrive. When I'm traveling or thriving or having a really good hair day, you better believe that I'll be posting that too. I just want people who are having a tougher time to not feel that they have to coat their struggles behind a facade that all is perfect. That can be damaging and isolating and I would rather be there through the hard spaces of life than to not know that they existed at all.

I recently was at a friend's house that I hadn't seen in a while. He asked how I was doing and I gave my automatic response, I was good. And he said, "No... really. How are you really?" And I started crying. There were tears that I didn't even realize needed to be released. There is beauty in being in a space where you feel comfortable enough to unpeel your layers. It is okay to shed your armor of how you think you should be perceived in the world. Don't let the comparison of people on the internet steal your happiness. Don't compare their edited filters of a trip of a lifetime to your everyday real world outtakes. Own your life for better and for worse and raise a glass to your authentic journey. Chances are they have experienced the hard too. I know they do. Anytime I write about the challenges of marriage or parenting or life or grief, I receive messages that say yes... I thought it was just me... I know... me too...

me too... and isn't connection what brought us all here in the first place?
You can still find me on Facebook, Twitter and Instagram (sorry LinkedIn). But more than anything else, I hope that you'll find me in real life.

Imperfect and unfiltered.
Cheers.

A dear friend of mine said the most
beautiful thing that I can't stop
thinking about. I told her that
sometimes it felt like my rock
bottom had a trap door. And she
said to me to just keep looking for
the ladders. The people that we
choose to give our time and energy
to, just make sure that they are the
ladders. Not the ones that push us
down further. That is it: just keep
looking for the ladders. It is as
simple and as complicated as that.
But my God, I am so crazy grateful
for the ladders in my life. Here's to
the dreamers and the lifters and
the angels among us. In all the
hard and the dark in this world,
there will always be ladders as
long as we keep remembering to look
for them. As long as we keep
remembering to be them.

Here's to going upward.

Dear Girls and Boys of the World,

There are a few things that I think you need to know. The things
that you aren't going to find in a textbook or a church or maybe
even your own home. There is power in the dos and the don'ts in
this world. And it is imperative to know the difference.

Don't apologize for your wildness.
Don't apologize for your voice.
Or what makes you different.
Or what makes you the same.
Don't apologize for your style
And your smile
And all that makes you feel alive.
Don't apologize for saying no.
Or yes.
Don't ignore your gut instincts
Or the things that make the hair on your neck stand tall
Or the things that make you feel fear before any other emotion.
There is an endless strength in listening to what makes you afraid.
Please do not blanket your fear.
You are not alone.

If you have never felt at home in the body that you are born with
you can grant yourself the strength, courage and power to change it.
Your body is yours. Your mind is yours. Your soul is yours.
Love out loud so long as you love yourself first.
You owe nothing to anyone.
If no one listens do not give up.
Do. Not. Give. Up.
You have a voice and a choice
and you deserve to be heard.
Please don't apologize or make excuses for the people that weigh
you down and tear you apart.
It doesn't matter if this person is blood, honey or water.
They have no right.
You do.

Burying your own secrets has the power to break us.
And you have far more important things to break:
molds,

ceilings,
hearts,
expectations.
Own that voice.
Scream if you have to.
Whisper if you must.
Just don't be silent.
Be who you are.
Release the you that demands to be seen.

You are worthy of so much.
You are a spark in this world.
You bring the light.
You overcome the dark.
This is your time, your story, your stage.
Your life.

The world is ready for you.

Pretty is a lovely thing
to be called.

But have you tried out
bravery?

Pretty is the bones that
you are born with.

Brave is what you chose
to do with them.

Keep on Treading Tribe

I used to see the piles of clothes strewn in every corner of every room and feel helpless. Tears welled. My shaken voice would raise. Those clothes were an exact representation of the failure that I felt as a mother. Growing mountains of messy, all consuming guilt. Wash, dry, fold, put away, get muddy, outgrow, buy more, pass on, change seasons, repeat. Never ending piles. Never put away. Never ahead of anything at all. The treading everyday life of parenthood. Each day repeating itself. Never getting any closer to shore. Just (barely) keeping my head above water. Maybe one minute gaining inches forward only to have the flu or teething or a tantrum in aisle two to push me back farther back than I felt I even began.

I have a dear friend who is pregnant with twins. She texted me a picture of her bare beautiful belly. Her skin glowed with the badges of motherhood; the marks of growth that feels too big to contain. Her belly button protruding just enough as if to say *two stunning lives are growing here and we just need to make more room for them; they need every centimeter of valuable real estate possible.* I used to have that same belly button; those same badges of a mother's work and honor. You get amnesia of all the "wise" words strangers say to you in public when you are pregnant but one comment I will never forget is a five year old whispering to her sibling, "I can see the baby's nose." Some of my most favorite words ever.

Now that all four of my babes are in school I have that glorious pleasure of going to the grocery store alone. Some may view these trips as a chore but I find them to be a blissful vacation- all that gorgeous food, oh so many options! How lucky are we to live in this land of being able to create any recipe you dream and to do it within driving distance? LOVE. And to go to this place without having to strap anyone in and without constant requests for snacks and more snacks and high fructose corn syrup and to be alone with my own thoughts and time and recipes is borderline orgasmic for me. Which is why on a recent Trader Joe's solo trip, I couldn't help but to be surprised when I stopped and stared at a mother in the trenches. She had a baby in a Bjorn that had just traded in its newborn wails to succumb to sleep on her chest. A two year old hung off the cart in cowboy boots opening another mozzarella stick while a four year old in an Elsa gown followed behind driving an overflowing little red cart recklessly colliding with the sample station. That momma was forgetting what it feels like to breathe. I showed her that her haven was near; there is a free coffee sample station as well. She smiled, poured a cup and breathed it in like it was a cappuccino poured on an Italian countryside.

I am you I thought. No that's not true. *I was you.* But I am still part of your tribe. The surviving motherhood tribe. The tribe that in the thick of it all is barely treading to stay afloat and never goes to the bathroom alone and too often forgets how to breathe. The this-is-so-insanely-hard-why-don't-people-talk-about-how-insanely-hard-it-is place in life.

And in a blink it evolves. It is still insanely hard but at least you can shower alone. And sometimes you have a moment to think and eat warm food and breathe. And you remember in awe what it felt like to have life flutter inside of you. And to have a newborn fall asleep on you. And to have cowboys and princesses accompany you to the store. And that is why strangers give you that sympathetic "I've been there" stare and the "please please enjoy it" hand gestures. It is not out of jealousy or meaning to be rude or longing to restart that journey. *Oh hell no.* It is because we are all part of that same tribe and sweet love it will get easier. You will wear your badges with pride. And you will realize, perhaps not in the moment that you most need to, but in a moment of being alone in a store looking at a mirror of the past and see, truly see, that motherhood is consuming and exhausting and just may be the most important work of your life.

The pure irony of it all is that there are endless days that you are going to want to fast forward only to look back and wished that you had hit the pause button.

So now I'm hitting pause and looking at the piles upon piles of

clothes drying by the basement fire and thinking *how lucky am I?*
We were blessed to have a two hour delay this morning and there
was nowhere we had to be like all of the other mornings and so my
kids went out in the snow. They are grown enough to zip up their
own coats and young enough to feel like they are flying when they
sled down our hill. Bliss.

If you are treading, please keep on keeping on. And please
remember that there are lifeboats in the form of girlfriends and
coffee and babysitters and even the woman (creepily) staring at you
at the store. Ask for help if you need it. There is no shame in it. You
are not alone. This tribe is for life.

Xo

You
Get
This
One
Life.

That's it.

If you are waiting for a
sign to start living it,
this is for you.

#thetimeisrightnow

37 Things That I Have Learned in 37 Years

We get so caught in the weight of the everyday and we wait for big milestone days to make a change and break the cycle. We wait for the weekend to have fun, for New Years to make a resolution, for our 30th/40th/50th birthdays to make bolder life choices. I don't want to wait for my life to begin anymore. We can break the cycle, beginning now, even when we have so much more to learn.

I am 37 years old and here are 37 things that I know right now:

1. Life is tough. You are tougher.

2. Being brave and kind cost nothing and can shape everything.

3. It is never too late.

4. Hearing a child laugh is the greatest sound in the world.

5. Chase light. Chase dreams. Chasing people is not what you were born to do.

6. There is nothing that you cannot accomplish when you put on lip gloss, mascara and a great pair of shoes.

7. Settling does not look good on anyone.

8. It is okay to fake it until you make it.

9. It is okay to be in love with a well-placed swear word.

10. Some people will drill holes in your life boat. Stop making room for them to stay on board.

11. Girlfriends are the best therapy.

12. Learn the power of the word no.

13. Having to mourn someone who is still alive will be one of the most difficult things that you have to do in this life.

14. Your gut does not lie. Listen to it.

15. Linger longer with people who see your worth. The believers and the joy seekers. The people that want to laugh with you at your kitchen table and they do not care how dirty the floor is beneath them.

16. When in doubt, just keep dancing.

17. Not everyone deserves your time and energy and to be told your best stories. Not everyone deserves a place at your tea party.

18. The world does not benefit from you living a life of fear.

19. Put on your own oxygen mask first.

20. The body is the house to the soul. Nourish it, protect it, celebrate it.

21. Stop apologizing for the things that you have had no control over.

22. Confidence is sexy. Smart wit is sexier.

23. You can change your life at any given moment. You have options even when you think that you don't. If you are miserable, that is all the justification that you need to write a new chapter. Stop waiting for external bruises and the perfect season of your life to align to make a change. If you wait, it may never happen. And you will wake up and be 20 years older and every bit as unhappy. Trust yourself. Trust your strength. If people can't understand that, please see #10.

24. Perfection and comparison are overrated, draining and are the thieves of joy.

25. Dress up for yourself. Dress up because it is Tuesday. Show up for your life. Dress for it, even when you don't want to. Especially when you don't want to. There is a time for pajamas of course. But the daylight needs your tigress ways.

26. You have enough time for what matters.

27. If someone is clawing at the door to get out of your house, do not turn the deadbolt to keep them in. Do not contain them. Turn the handle, love. You have the courage to set them and yourself free.

28. Embrace your mistakes. They make you beautiful, strong and deliciously human.

29. Tell the people that you love that you love them. Write it down. Repeat.

30. Travel. Read more books. Keep your eyes and soul open. Take some risks even if you are a grown up, especially if you are a grown up. You have a pulse, live accordingly.

31. Whisper. Scream. Roar. Trust your magnificent voice.

32. Let go of the things not meant for you. This is not limited to, but does include guilt, dear mommas.

33. Allow yourself three times to complain about something. After that you either need to make a change. Or you need to stop complaining. It is as simple and as complicated as that.

34. Breathe. Unplug. Smile. Be caught being happy, present and awake.

35. Surround yourself with those that care less about how they show their lives on social media and more about how they show up in their real lives.

36. Your children need to see you rise. Everyday. You are not their puppet. You are not their best friend. Teach respect and kindness and how to make their own peanut butter and jelly sandwiches. Show them how to rise even on the dark days. And they will too.

37. You get one life. That is it. Make yourself proud.

SPRING

You Are Not Just a Mother

I need a favor from you, queen bee. I need you to stop saying that
you are "just" a mother. I need you to stop right now. I need you to
stop saying it in your future. Your child is so much more than just.
Your life is more than just. You are so far beyond just... just doesn't
deserve you.

Here is what you are (*just* in case you need the reminder):

You are
strong
stunning
amazing
nurturing
powerful
bold
a hope
a light
a vault
a believer
a dreamer
a warrior
the love
the glue
the confetti
the future.

And this is what you do (again and again and again):

you chauffeur
you work
you pay
you cook
you clean
you fold
you teach
you build
you create
you laugh
you play

you call
you answer
you listen
you speak
you inspire
you believe
you remember
you release
you forgive
you endure
you hold
you lift
you climb
you carry
you glow
you dream
you sacrifice
you cry
you bleed
you bandage
you spill open

you show up.

There is nothing slight about it. There is nothing just about it. You do not have time for the justs, the justifications and the judgements. You are doing the best that you can. And you are killing it.
Rock on momma.
You are extraordinary.
Thank you for showing up.

Cheers to us.

Love...

You are so much
stronger

and more resilient

and more courageous

than you could ever
give yourself credit
for.

Please please please

don't forget that.

#youarestrength

Yes. My Hands Are Full.

Strangers say oh so many things when I'm out in public with all of my children. "Are they all yours?" Yes. "Are they identical twins?" No. There is a key part of their anatomy that makes boy/girl twins not identical. I've been asked if I needed a nanny. Or a television. But without a second thought the #1 most commonly spoken stranger comment is (drumroll please...), "Your hands sure are full."

I'm told this almost every time we go out in the world. Sometimes several times in one outing. I can't even imagine how the Kate plus Eight (back when the eight were small and John was in the title) ever even made it through anywhere. I know people mean well but it is a somewhat exhausting comment. Exhausting really because I could never come up with a witty or even semi-witty response. When the twins were babies and I was schlepping them around in a double stroller, two grocery carts or sometimes some variation of one in a baby Bjorn and the other in a sling with my older two by my sides, I typically gave a sleep-deprived "yes." Or an unspoken forced smile with desperation in my eyes.

Where does my latte go?

As time marched on and more sleep was had by all, the well-meaning strangers would still say it again and again "You sure have your hands full" and I would try my best lines on them like a comedian, trying to gage their reactions of whether my response worked or not. I tried, "You should see my laundry room" or a simple truth, "I drink a lot of wine." Sometimes a dramatic *"HELP ME"* seemed to go over well.

After almost nine years of parenting and four years of surviving these twins, I think I've finally found the right response. It's not witty, might even be borderline cheesy but it is the truth. And I love honesty. Here goes:

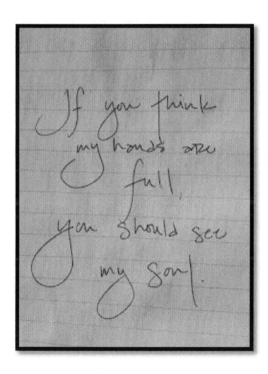

Every day I'm in awe that
my momma raised the four of
us without the help of
Google.

Amazing.

#howdidshedoit #thanksmom

So...What are You Doing With Your Life?

When Lucy was my only baby which feels so long ago that I may have dreamt that whole beautiful space in time, I was completely enamored with being a mother. I really rocked it. I would put her in a sling or a Bjorn or some other Zen type of bundle that kept her within centimeters of my skin. AT. ALL. TIMES. We would explore the world by day, read endless "Goodnight Moon" by night and dine on organic homemade baby food in between. I could have been a cover model for Earth Mother, Zen Child Magazine. Does that exist? It really should have a decade ago before I had bags under my eyes.

I never felt that I had to justify that time, I was too in love with it. I never felt that a lack of a paycheck made me less of something. I felt that if I was happy and Lucy was happy and even (bonus!) Big Daddy was happy than what did it even matter?

I think in addition to having firmer skin that I was actually a lot smarter then.

Fast forward to yesterday morning. 9 year old Lucy and 7 year old Niko are crying and having an all-around ridiculous moment over who is supposed to be cleaning the litter box, 4 year old Micah somehow managed to smear his own feces all over the toilet seat and 4 year old Sophia is ~~screaming~~ serenading "Let it Go" to Willie (Nilly) Nelson who is trying claws out and desperate to hide (I'm with you cat). We have 13 minutes to get all this shit (literally) cleaned up before we will need to put on 18 layers of clothing because it is 18 degrees in "spring" and sprint to the bus because there is no way in hell I'm strapping them all in and driving this entourage to school this frozen day. And one of these children who shall not be named because they are normally angelic but this child said these words while hysterically crying out loud to me, *"Could you please just help us for once in your life?"*

Ummmm... excuse me?

The mom face I gave her could have won an award. No words needed to be spoken. Not that that stopped me from speaking them.

Yes. I am so blessed. And lucky. Yes I know. And of course mo' kids means mo' problems and less money, energy and patience to go around. I need not complain. I really am happy and my kids amaze me every single day. The mornings are not normally filled with so much crap clean-up anymore. But that doesn't mean that it's not challenging. And here is the ironic thing: I now feel like I really have to justify my time and staying at home. Why? Why do we feel the need to prove ourselves? Because I have two kids in school and my twins are in preschool? That means that I have maybe four hours a week when I'm not volunteering and doing all of the craziness motherhoodness that I can go to a store alone. Pick a store, any store and it will be a marvelous experience when you fly it solo. I went to K-Mart today and felt like Martha Stewart herself. Yes, I got some self-tanning lotion and new hand towels. BOOM. Look out summer.

Next fall all four kids will get on a bus (let's hope it's the right one) and be gone all the live long day. That is what I already feel the need to justify. I feel like a senior in high school with people asking what my plan in next year and you really want to say something confident and awesome like "Yale. I have a full ride to Yale." But the truth is I really just want and need to take a year off to think and figure it all out for a bit because for the first time in a long time I will be given a space to breathe and think.

But we don't usually say those really honest things out loud. We feel that we need to be needed and to do and to be more. Always. We are all judgers of time, our own and everyone else's for better or worse. So what do I really want to do with my life, next year and always?

I want to write and read and teach and take yoga. And occasionally go and read to my kids classes. And then roll out of there and listen to what quiet feels like inside of my house. And think. And save the world. And be so happy and refreshed and greet them with wide open arms when they get home. And be that Zen patient mother again. And drink wine. That is what I want.

In t-shirt form it would be:
Yoga. Write. Wine.

And on the back it would read: **And Save the World**. But I do think if we all do those things on the front, the saving the world would be a whole lot more on its way.

But somehow that didn't seem like enough to say out loud so these are the ideas that I've seriously thrown out to Big Daddy as potential jobs:

- Yoga Studio Owner
- Open a Coffee House
- Open a Wine Bar
- Chicken Raiser
- Real Estate Agent
- Bestselling Author (why not just shoot right for the top?)
- Seamstress (I don't even know how to sew)
- Open a Boutique (by the sea of course)
- Open a Yoga Studio, Coffee House, Wine Bar in One
- Key Chain Maker (is that a job?)
- Tea Towel Maker (definitely not a job but that hasn't stopped me from hoarding towels to applique)
- Or we could just run away to an island...

I never realized how patient my husband was until I just typed all of that out. It's really only a sample of job or whatever-they-are possibilities that have ran through my mind over the last several weeks.

My brother Tim gave me the best answer ever about what his wife was going to do with her time. They live in South Korea where daycare is free (*say what?!* It's true- it really is) and she was going to put her beautiful two year old twins in the program a couple of mornings a week.
Me: AMAZING. This is so exciting. What is Lena going to do during that time (see even I ask because I'm just so freakin curious)?
Tim: She's always wanted to take some yoga classes so that's what she's going to do.
Me: BRILLIANT. She so deserves that.

It never occurred to him or to her that she didn't.

I'm going to change what I say from here on out when people ask me what I am going to do with myself next year. I know people ask with good well-meaning intention, it is me who is on the defense of my time. But from now on I'm going to own it and say with pride: Yoga, Write, Wine. And maybe point to it in t-shirt form. Hhhhmmmm...T-shirt maker has job potential. *Kidding. Sort of.*

Whatever we do, let's own it. And if you are feeling like you are "just" a mom, please remember this: there is nothing just about it.

Keep on keeping on hard working mommas and poppas...
It feels like wine time...
Cheers.

Some days I make green
smoothies or gluten free
homemade banana muffins
for my kids.

This morning they had
Doritos at 8 a.m.

#balance

A Peace Offering to End the Parent Wars

Stay at home moms/dads vs. working moms/dads. Who has it harder? The honest answer is that we all do. I have yet to meet a parent who would describe parenting as easy. And if that parent does exist, could you be a doll and come over to my house around 5 p.m.? I could really use an extra set of hands.

We are all trying to do the best that we possibly can. It is as simple and as complicated as that. Whether you work outside or inside of the home, chances are that you have had to justify your decision to someone. Or at the very least, or shall I say, most, you have had to justify it to yourself. We have had to convince ourselves that whether or not we receive a paycheck, that what we are doing is the best choice for our children, our partners and our lifestyles. Shouldn't we be the best judges of what is best for our own families without the criticism and judgment of society? Or worse, to hear that harsh discernment from our dear amazing, hard-working and rarely ever thanked fellow mothers? If that is the case, then momma really does *not* know best.

I have had the joy and sacrifice of staying at with our four children. One thing that is an absolute reality- there have been days that I would have given at least three of my limbs to have been able to trade places with my husband and work his excruciatingly stressful career (in particular, after our twins were born). The other reality is that I know that there are moments that he would do the absolute same to trade places with me (in particular, the one future day that the twins will be in school).

Both jobs are beyond challenging and the argument of who has it worse is beyond exhausting. What if instead of focusing on the grunt work of it all, that we focus more on the pure hope of it all? What if we focused our energies on supporting one another and being there to unleash to one another when we've had a crazy, hide in the bathroom-because-it-has-a-lock type of day? We teach our children to love and respect one another, regardless of gender, race or religion. So it is now time for us to do the same for each other, to show the respect we so deserve, regardless of job status.

Whether running the boardroom, the bedroom or the PTA, chances are the parents in our lives are bending over backwards for someone else besides ourselves. Instead of questioning how we are or are not utilizing our degrees, maybe we should thank one another. Or at least, offer each other a hug with a side of espresso. Without doubt or question, we have both earned it.

A May Love Note

I still have moments when I feel
like I'm drowning. I know I
shouldn't. But I do. Because it
doesn't always get easier; it evolves
into another place with high
expectations. There is so much
running around you that forget to
breathe. I am so ready for all of
the sports to be finished and all of
the commitments of school and
lunches and reading logs and
making projects with hot glue and
homework to be finished. I'm not so
much ready for the kids to be all
up in my grill again but to have
open days and open nights and
nowhere in particular that we have
to be. That is bliss. And ironically
it is the same thing that I had
when they were tiny and I felt like
I was drowning in a different type
of way. Oh motherhood, you are one
crazy bitch how you turn those
tables. So in the in between and the
trying to wrap up all of the things
that need to happen in these next
few weeks, if you stumble upon a
love letter that one of those wild
ones wrote and hid it among the
chaos of your office with no other
intention than to make you smile,
allow yourself to do that.

Smile. Breathe. Repeat.

Know that you are loved deeper than you will ever realize.

We got this.

Praise for the Child that Doesn't Get Straight A's

Yesterday was report card day for us. Lucy looks forward to this day like most kids look forward to Christmas. The countdown *(two more weeks- eek!)*, the anticipation *(I couldn't eat lunch today, I was just too excited to get my report card)* and the victory *(YES- I got straight A's- Principal's Honor Roll!!!)*. This was the first year that Niko got letter grades and he is definitely one that thrives more when he knows he's getting graded on something and he, too, got straight A's. This is the first year that the twins have been in school, let alone the first report card, no perfect marks or even close to it, but they did excel in the attendance department.

I am ridiculously proud of all of them.

When Lucy was a baby, I wasted far too much time comparing her to other babies. *When will she sleep through the night? When will she start rolling? Why isn't she rolling? Why isn't she crawling/walking/talking yet when the other babes at Gymboree class are?* I wished her older far too quickly instead of just soaking in each place in life that she gloriously was. She was healthy and happy so why was I even wishing for more than that? I was stealing joy from both of us to be caught up in someone else's timeline. And it continues as they get older: the comparison. When are kids are great at school, we want them to be better at sports. If they are natural athletes, we want them to get better grades. When they are great at musical instruments, we wish them to be better at helping around the house. Amazing artists, let's work harder at math. More activities, more lessons, more tutoring, more foreign languages, more sports, more camps, more training, more scouts, more dance... more, more, more to exceed unrealistic expectations that we put on them.

Enough. The quest for perfection in our children so that we feel better about ourselves is exhausting. We miss the opportunity to embrace the imperfection in us all and the beautiful gifts that we all bring to the table. I'm not saying that children shouldn't be pushed to work harder and practice and read and study and be reminded to make their beds every single day; they absolutely should. That is why we are parents and the big challenging responsibility is to make our children the most wonderful human beings possible. But that means that they don't need to do it all perfectly. It means showing up and to have the courage to do it all over again every single day.

My mother-in-law gave me some of the best parenting advice that I've ever heard:
Everyone brings their own recipe to the world.

Take a moment to think of your own recipe that you bring to the world. Now think of your child's. It doesn't have to be in the form of a textbook or the number of soccer goals scored. Or something that we can even put on a college application or a resume.

Lucy is reading. And loving school.
Niko is building and creating and imagining.
Micah can figure out how so many things work. He has an engineer's mind that boggles mine.
And Sophia. Sophia can make a friend wherever she goes.
She tells me "My heart is as big as my whole body."

Yes it is. And kindness, the unconditional eye opening kind, is a recipe that will serve her endlessly in this life. She might not ever get straight A's and that is completely okay.
She shows up and she makes the world bright. I will take it.

Not all things in life should be measured in the form of report cards.
Shine on warriors...

Motherhood can be a thankless job. But sometimes you get these moments that are so much better than what you could have ever imagined them to be.

Last night when I checked on the kids who were fast asleep, I noticed Micah's blanket was on the floor. I covered him back with it and with his eyes closed he curled back up into it and exhaled a tiny, "Thank you Momma."

He never opened his eyes. He just knew it was me.

Maybe that's the best kind of thank you. A love that doesn't have to be witnessed to know it exists... it's there, unconditional and relentless.

So to all the mommas out there, even when you think you are invisible, even when you don't think you are heard, even when you repeat the same tasks again and again and again... you are felt. You are seen. You are adored.

Keep on keeping on rockstars.

#mommasrock

A Love Letter to my Mother-in-Law

Dearest Yia-Yia...

I feel like there are too many things that I haven't told you. I think that is the thing with super women. We just assume that they know how extraordinary their super powers are that we forget to voice them out loud. We forget that everyone needs to have their cup refilled (yes, your exact words that you've said to me). I think it is beyond time that I expressed my gratitude out loud for the way you love out loud. There aren't enough words or pages for all of the things so here is just a beginning.

You love my children. You say yes to them and dedicate whole days to the word yes. They know Yia-Yia is synonymous with laughter and play and swinging and all that is important in childhood. And adulthood. Whenever I am in doubt about the right decision of how to handle a situation with my kids I usually ask myself *What Would Yia-Yia do?* And that always finds a way to bring me to the right path; the happier path; the path of yes.

You love me. You love me like I was one of your own children which makes me feel like one of the luckiest girls in the world. You have been a therapist, a friend and a mother. You not only watch my children but you have slipped me money when I've gone out the door for girls weekends. You give the best gifts from shoes to clothes to Anthropologie happiness. I know love has nothing to do with the material but I am astonished by the thought behind each and every thing. I know that I haven't thanked you enough because I am the worst ever at thank you cards, but I know your generosity is lined in it all. I myself am stitched together by flaws laced in hopeful intentions but you never point them out. You never make me feel like I'm not enough but instead like I am a light and I am not alone. You have an understated way of making everyone feel like they have gifts in this world that need to be shined for all to see. You see all of our children's strengths, all of their gifts. Not to say that they don't each have their faults, of course they do, but what a hopeful world it is to just look for the good. That in itself is a gift of yours. It is not a slight thing to be able to see everyone's light.

You've shown me the love that is food. And that there isn't a situation in life that couldn't be improved by a glass of Chardonnay.

You are a brilliant, bountiful and beautiful chef. You make the type of food that people yearn to be in your kitchen. You provide the company that people don't want to leave. And when they do they will not leave empty handed. I have not left your kitchen without at least 3 Tupperware containers of your delicious food in the last 15 years.

You've given me your son. He is of course both of ours, for better or worse and I still call dibs on you should we ever get a divorce but when we got married, you handed him to me with grace. You handed him to me with hope. He will always be one of the best people I will ever meet in this world and that is to your credit. He is a strong man and he was raised by a strong woman. I am in awe of the tenacity in those genes and am grateful that blood that thick is coursing through my children.

And there is you. Resilience personified. You take nothing lying down and you take it with a smile. You find humor in what others would hide from. You bring laughter with a side of spanakopita. Dirty jokes with wine. Strength with spirit. You do not let things break you. You overcome.

I hope that when I become a mother-in-law that I do half as good a job as what you have done for me. That would be the ultimate success. I know I never have called you Mom but that doesn't mean that I would ever consider you as anything else. Thank you. Thank you for everything. You will always be more than I could hope for.

Love you.
Always.

*update for you: I wrote this over a year ago for my amazing
mother-in-law. At that point, she had battled cancer three times.
And then, late last fall it came back for a fourth time.

On a Tuesday afternoon in June she passed away.

When I told my children that she had died they said they couldn't
imagine a world without her in it, all I could say was, "I know. I
know."

There was only one her. And my God, she is missed.

I'll see you on the other side of the stars, Ang. Love you like wild.

The Obituary for Yia-Yia

Angela Stavrou Moore, age 67 of Bel Air, MD, warrior, food lover and selfless human passed away on June 20, 2017. She will always be known to her children and grandchildren as the world's greatest Yia-Yia.

Angie could never let a great pun or a great opportunity to cook an amazing meal for her family (whether they were hungry or not) pass her by. She was born thirty seconds after her twin sister Nikki to a passionate Greek, Nickolaos Stavrou and a fierce Italian, Rose Stavrou. She became the funny and fearless big sister to her siblings Linda, Dorian, Aletha, Stephen and Mark.

She met her husband John Moore at the University of Maryland where they not only became proud Terp fans and alumni, but two of the most thoughtful parents of all time to their three exceptional children, Nicole, Stephen, and Andrew, where she instilled roots, relentless wit, and a lifetime love of the beach and all foods that include feta.

In addition to being the family's best chef, her perseverance as an advocate for children throughout her entire career as a social worker could earn her the status of a saint. And when her children got married to Travis, Katie, and Courtney, respectively, her angel wings only grew wider and she never treated them as anything less than her own children. But of all the joy of her world, it was her grandchildren, Lucy, Luke, Niko, Jake, Sophia, Micah, Max, Charis and Penny that stole her heart.

If someone could survive on their will to live alone, she would have lived forever, which her dear friends and family selfishly hoped

would have happened. But what a time they
had while she was here.

Services and the party she wanted will be
held at 3:00 p.m.
In lieu of flowers she would have wanted you
to share a beautiful meal with your family.

Dear Friend Who Has Lost Someone That They Love,

Hi there.

I know that people are blanketing you with words like "I'm sorry" right now because they just don't know what else to say. I wish I had the right words to offer you. All I know is that there are aches attached to grief that can never be healed. Sometimes there are no right words, no right explanation. Sometimes life is not fair. Sometimes there is a loss so deep that part of our pulse is taken with it. Sometimes there are no Band-Aids. Sometimes there is no solution; no quick fix; no miracle cure. Sometimes all we need is time. Sometimes we know that time will never be enough. Sometimes we need people to say that they are here; that they aren't going anywhere. And if you need someone to remember, I will remember with you. If you need to be seen, I will see you.
I know you sometimes catch yourself feeling like yourself again. And you know that it is fleeting. Sometimes you will catch yourself smiling or laughing and that will be followed by an avalanche of guilt. You will feel bad when you are not living, you will feel bad when you are. Guilt will sometimes be served with a side of guilt.
I know that you are treading carefully right now. I know that sometimes it feels like it takes all that you have to keep your head above water. I know what it feels like to be submerged. I know how hard it is to rise above the surface, how hard it can be to work for every inhale. Your grief will come to you in waves. There will be waves that you can name as if they are low tide and high tide, like anger and a deep sadness. And ones that are harder to name, harder to brace yourself for their impact. Confusion, denial and hopelessness will blindside you and try to take you under.
My dear friend, please just keep treading. Keep riding the inevitable waves. Stamp your feet down with rage, scream at the sky, shed tears in the deep, bury yourself in the sand if you need to, just keep a space that keeps you breathing. Keep the space that keeps you awake. Keep the space that keeps you feeling. Keep your head toward the sun and in due time you will feel its warmth again. Take all the time that you need. When it comes to healing, there should never be a stopwatch involved.
And know this above all else: I am here. I will hold your hand in the ocean. I will hold it in the sand. I won't let go. And if you need to

escape, you can always climb in my lifeboat. There will always be a space for you. You are not alone.

I am so sorry.

I am here.

Always.

It's 8 pm and I'm at our third lacrosse event of the night. I'm particularly in love with this one because it's for my oldest daughter and it's cold and I get to be alone in a warm car (i.e. bliss).

But there's a head coach out there on this windy night who happens to coach four other lacrosse teams. He doesn't even have a daughter on our team. He just loves the game and the community and is invested in a future that has strong female athletes in it. He's amazing. So to every coach out there who loves a game and teaches a child and believes in the power of being a part of a team and gives up not only their 8 o'clock personal hour but an endless number of hours on top of that, please know that we see you.

Thank you. Thank you. Thank you.

#coachesrock

An Imperfect Love Letter to my Kids

I know that I tell you I love you an endless number of times a day. I know I also raise my voice too much and I'm grumpy before I have had caffeine and I have high expectations of you and all of that is probably never ever going to change. So please remember this: I am beyond proud of you. I am overwhelmed with the luck that you were born to me. And I know that I don't tell you that enough.

Here are just some of the reasons of why my soul could burst with pride:

Because sometimes you say please and thank you without me having to ask you to.

Because you have a laugh that is stunning and contagious.

Because you sometimes remember to not pick your nose in the living room.

Because you are so kind.

Because if I wasn't your parent, I'd want to be the type of friend you'd want to have a sleepover with.

Because you sometimes choose to go to the bathroom indoors. In a toilet.

Because I don't really mind when you go outside. I'd still want to have a sleepover.

Because you show up.

Because you sometimes sleep until after 6:30 in the morning.

Because you don't mind when dirt is under your fingernails.

Because you keep on trying.

Because you are okay with wearing mismatched socks when I'm behind on laundry.

Because your heart is so big it can barely be contained in your body.

Because you appreciate the greatness that is an ice cream sundae.

Because you live out loud.

Because you help clean the bathrooms.

Because you love books.

Because you aren't perfect.

Because you know that I'm not either.

Because you've taught me more than I thought I was capable of learning.

Because you know that success isn't measured in dollars.

Because you know that joy isn't either.

Because you give the type of hugs that make me forget to exhale.

Because you are stubborn. Like your father.

Because you are smart. Like me.

Because you love a good party.

Because you run so fast when you get off the bus, like the front door can't come quickly enough.

Because you remind me to stop taking it all so seriously.

Because you draw and build and dance.

Because you see opportunity in a rainy Saturday.

Because you can dream things that the world needs.

Because you are light.

Because you are the future.

Because you have set fire to the past.

Because you have made my present.

Because of you, I know what pride is. I know what happy feels like.
And I get to be awakened and blanketed by all that is good.
Every. Single. Day.

I love you. I am proud of you. For all that you do... thank you.

Always.
Momma

90% of me telling my kids
I'm looking for their
uniform, I'm pulling it
out of the dirty clothes,
spraying it with
Febreeze and throwing it
in the dryer. Then I ask
them if they have
checked the dryer.

Boom.

#parentingwin

What She Really Wants for Mother's Day

Years ago when my oldest daughter was three and my middle son was one I woke up on Mother's Day beaming with anticipation of what this day would hold in store, this celebration of all the craziness of motherhood, to be thought of and be shown gratitude for this thankless life's work, if for only this one day. I tiptoed to the kitchen, our unofficial home of all things celebratory, to see what my amazing husband would have on display for me. To my ~~shock disappointment mouth dropped open with confusion and fear for him~~ surprise, nothing was there. Not a thing. No card. No flowers. No breakfast. No construction paper stamped with cute little hands. Not even a mimosa for goodness sake. Zilch for the woman who gave birth to his children.

Me: Um babe... were you planning on doing something for Mother's Day?
Babe: I thought Mother's Day is the day to celebrate my mother.
Me: But... I'm a mom. Our children are too young to know that this day exists. They need you to help them.
Babe. Oh...whoops.
Me: (instant sobbing, blubbering mess) Do you not think I'm a good mother... it's the one day I get recognized for being slightly good at anything at all... and I'm going to be forty (at the time this was 12 years away)...
and so on and so on. It was not pretty.
Babe: Why don't you go shopping and you can buy whatever you want?
Me: (able to dry the tears but still feeling like a woman scorn) Okay.

This was a wonderful consolation prize but let's just say that my husband has never again forgotten that I am a mother on Mother's Day. Men, do not be like this. Do not forget the woman who has brought your children into the world. What hurt all the more was that Steve (babe/husband) is usually so thoughtful and the best gift giver, his fault was that he didn't recognize this as a day that should be celebrated for me. Side note: I am the one who buys the gift for his mother so please don't picture him making her a soufflé. If he had just written on a card on the kitchen table that he would watch the kids so that I could go shopping, all would have been glorious.

Sweet mother of all things holy,
don't forget her on Mother's Day.

I am going to let you in on a secret that should in no way even be a
secret. There are three keys to keeping a woman happy (another
bonus, all are free): **attention, affection and appreciation**. It really
is that simple and yet so many women would reveal that those three
needs are not being met in her life. My husband actually told me on
one of our first dates that his best friend's dad gave him that bit of
advice that those three things are essential to a woman's happiness.
It stunned me. I'm not sure that I've ever heard more glorious words
of wisdom.

Think about it. If you grant her those three things she will be all the
more inclined to fulfill the three keys to your happiness (which let
me know if I'm off-base but I believe they may be sex, food and
more sex).

Here is the breakdown: if she is talking, listen to her and
acknowledge her thoughts (attention, check). Hold her hand if you
are walking together. Embrace her when you see her. Hold her with
no other pretense than to let her feel what it feels like to be held
(affection, check). Now appreciation may be the hard one for many
but it is so essential for her self-esteem and well-being. You need to
voice out loud that she is amazing. A reminder of why you chose

her out of all the women in this world is always a great thing. Tell her she is beautiful. Tell her that her spaghetti and her spaghetti covered children are the best. Tell her that you love her. And that you are the lucky one (appreciation, check).

The more confidence that you help to instill in her, the more confidence that she will carry. And that my friends is a very sexy quality. Which makes it all full circle and the whole house will be happy. That is the perfect mother's day gift. So write it in a card and while you are at it, give her a day to herself, shopping spree optional but time alone essential. Let her choose the day because after all the triple A's you will be throwing her way she may want to spend time with her kids and with you baby daddy on Mother's Day (but if she wants to choose that day, don't hold it against her; she hasn't been alone in eight years). Time allows her to fall in love with herself again which is necessary for all the love she gives to her children and all the gratitude she holds for you.

And what comes around goes around. Father's day is just around the corner...

Here's hoping that all
you Mommas get a
reminder that you are
math skills are on point,
you are as pretty as a
shouting star and that
you have a day full of
laughter. And kissing.
And mimosas.

#happymothersday
#sorrymatthew

y Mom has a pretty smile! I like to make her smile by
Kissing her

y Mom is as pretty as a _shouting star_

Mom is smart! She even knows $1 \div 1 = 1$ but
Matthew does not that.

ned _Micah_ Date _5-6-2016_

Merci Inventors of Ombre, Merci

I want to take a moment to thank those who invented the "ombre" hairstyle. Never has letting yourself go look so on trend. I like to think it was a mother or group of mothers who invented it. I heard it originated in France. This is how I imagine the whole situation going down:

A group of mothers are drinking wine one night at "book" club. They are commenting how they would love to go to the salon, alone, or get highlights or lowlights or something that looks like a hair style but they know the realization is that ain't nobody got time for that. Not yet. Not where they are in life.

When one momma, knee deep in Pinot Grigio, had a true eureka moment:
"Why don't we convince people that not going to the salon is stylish? Let's make people think that letting your highlights grow out 6 months past when you had a hair appointment to get them redone but little Jimmy got the stomach bug and now it is just not going to happen. That- that is the look that people should want to go for."
And another momma says with sheer joy, "Brilliant! All we need is one reality show star to get on board with it. It would help if we got a Kardashian. And the name. It just needs a good name."
One momma did a semester abroad in France 15 years ago but still obsesses about that time maybe a little too often, bursts out, "OMBRE! It means shadow en francais. Let's tell people that it started in Paris by models and they'll instantly be intrigued."
First drunk mom: "I'm pinning pictures of our hair right now to my ombre board."

They toasted their comedic genius and their already on trend grown out highlight hairstyle and the vision of ombre, thinking it would never get any further than this wine induced living room.

And then all it took was one Kardashian with an Instagram account. And then the millennials got on board. And Pinterest. Thank God. The pinning was unstoppable. Apparently brushing your hair is also now optional.

So thank you to the originators of ombre. Merci beaucoup. Let this trend last until I can get my wild, rebellious head of hair to a salon.

Cheers.

Before today we were so
close to making it
through the first
grade without one of
the twins making the
following confession:

"Mom, I ate glue today."

#soclose

Marriage. Is. Hard.

Can I just tell you something on the real and raw side? Marriage is hard. Insanely hard. There have been more moments in the last 11 years that have left me fragile and weak and broken that I would ever want to expose out loud. And you might not have ever experienced a moment in your "till death do us part" adventure that comes close to that. To which I would say to you friend "That is amazing. I hope you never do." But here is a truth in marriage (and definitely in parenting) you might not have reached your hard yet. You might not ever. But you may. And you're not alone. I think that is always okay to let one another know that we are not alone. Because that alone feeling can lead to many shades of darkness. And the thoughts that come under darkness are beyond frightening. So lets find the light. Together.

The reality is that marriage, to me, is like a roller coaster. Sometimes we just need to hold on and grip what we can. Sometimes we are up so high that we forget what it feels like to be down. And just as fast as that high came on, it all can come crashing down before you had a chance to brace yourself for it. And then there is the ripple effect of being up and down and spinning. You yell. You take it out on the kids. Or the dog. Or your cell phone provider. And that's when the septic system breaks and there's a car accident and someone gets sick and we are late to practice. And Christmas is just staring at you in the face alongside the Halloween decorations. And it all looks so horrendous together that you want to scream but remember that you have dignity so you open your bag of Reese's peanut butter pumpkins and you eat them with vengeance to show that you are on Team Halloween. Ha ha ha (insert evil Halloween laugh)...TAKE THAT TARGET!

That my friends is marriage. And life.

It rains sometimes. It is dark sometimes. And then it is light and beautiful and so full of future that you could just burst open. And it has the power to make you melt and crack then feel whole again once more.

And sometimes all it takes is breathing in that other person. And listening to them. And ~~turning off~~ muting the football game in the background. And getting out of the way of your own hurt so that you can listen to them. And to not instantly pounce on judgement or defense but to just listen wide open. To own your imperfection, not to just point out theirs.

Wine usually helps these conversations.

And you have two choices here: **to harden or to soften.** What outcome do you want? *To build a wall or to break one down.* It is as simple and as complicated as that. The softening isn't admitting defeat. It is saying: I choose you. I choose us. This day and maybe just maybe every day, just one day at once, I am going to pick you on this path. Our path. The softening just may be the key to the lasting.
Yesterday was my husband's 35th birthday. We met when we were 20 years old so we haven't yet grown old together but more trying to survive growing up to adulthood together. I usually try to write something (irritatingly) gushy and romantic for his birthday. But this day, nothing feels more romantic than to be real. And open. And to soften.
And to say:
I am ridiculously imperfect. And I'm sorry that I enjoy shopping so much. I'm sorry that I despise laundry. And I'm not so great at cleaning but amazing at procrastinating. And googling (it is an art, thank you). But I love to cook and laugh and sing loud when I don't know the words and I love to dance like the world depends on it and in my eyes that is not such a bad combination. And I choose you. Everyday. At the end of the day there is no one else that I want to dance with. Or laugh with. Or love out loud.

It is a choice to keep riding the ride.

Kindness
is
a
superpower.

Dear Mom,

Thank you is not enough.
It could never be enough.
But this is the only way to start a love letter written to you.

Thank you.

Thank you for being the most comforting human of all time.
Thank you for the bandages, for the cuts you witnessed and the
ones unseen that needed the most care of all. Thank you for the
decades of dinners and drives and laundry and the juggling and
the balancing and for making lemon meringue pie from scratch
with a side of unwavering questions from children at your feet.
Thank you for teaching compassion and empathy and for giving
my sister and I perms on Saturday nights. You taught us
strength, hope and class between curlers and warm brownies.
Thank you for teaching my brothers how to be good men. Thank
you for all that you sacrificed. Thank you for giving us a simple
delicious childhood and for letting us drink water straight from
the hose and for letting us play barefoot in the grass deep into the
dark night. You were the glue that held a world together and
expected nothing in return.
Thank you for building, bending and not breaking. Thank you
for teaching us when to speak and when to silence. You didn't
ask to be seen. But we saw you. We saw you. We saw your
grace. We saw you on the sidelines. We saw your silent tears at
the big life moments. We saw the dirt under your fingernails and
the laugh lines around your soft eyes. We saw you hold our own
children. We saw you carry those babies like the miracles that
they are. We saw in the quiver of your smile the reminder to hold
on while we still can because they grow up far too fast.
Thank you for your relentless belief in my joy. Not my success.
Not that you don't want to see that. But you've taught me that
happiness is the success. Kindness is the superpower. Creativity
is the beauty. Reading is the therapy. Intelligence is the radiance.
Listening is the art. Family is the love. Thank you for seeing
through the veil of my flaws. You see the fire and light in my

veins. Always have. Always will. I will never stop trying to make you proud. It is the least that I can do for you, dear being. You are a saint.

And I am so lucky to have been born to you.
I am so lucky Mom.

Thank you. For everything.
Always...

Coffee Shop Thoughts...

Life is so very short.
Wear the red heels. Be present. Take
a selfie in a faraway land and then
put your phone away. Say thank you
to your mother. Compliment a
stranger. Put a pen or paintbrush
to paper. Leave a mark. Tell a joke
to a child. Let a child tell you a
joke. Don't forget to laugh. Hold
someone's hand. Learn to forgive.
And let go. Listen to your gut. Love
yourself first. Find a way to move
your body every day. Read more
books. Create something with your
hands. Release yourself from guilt.
Tell the people you adore why you
adore them. Buy the coffee for the
person behind you.
Tomorrows are not infinite.
Live out loud. Now.
Celebrate what sings to your soul.
Now.
And smile.
Starting now.

The Girlfriend Vows

My dearest friends, I promise you this:

I promise to know when an occasion calls for ice cream or wine and the wisdom to know when it needs both.

I promise to be honest. Never brutal. Never painful. But to tell it like I'd like to be told.

I promise to be me. Broken, open, raw, vulnerable me.

I promise to accept you. Broken, open, raw, vulnerable you.

I promise to not vacuum before you come over. Unless it is almost a health code violation and it is in absolute dire need of it. Only then.

I promise to always be kind to the person that you are in love with. Even, and especially when, I don't think he/she deserves you.

I promise to be in your corner for your battles.

I promise to let you know when I am struggling through a battle of my own.

I promise to celebrate your victories.

I promise to never order a salad when we go out to eat. Unless it is followed by nachos.

I promise to love your children.

I promise to support your choices, mighty and small, even if they don't mirror mine.

I promise to laugh with you at all the appropriate times. And especially at the inappropriate ones.

I promise that when life is slippery and fragile and hurts too much to keep going forward that *you are not alone.*

I will be there. I will listen.
I will hold your hand.
I will dance with you.
I will cry with you.
I will toast with you.
And to you.

I will attempt to be all that you are to me.

I love you sister.
Always will.

Cheers to
hope,
joy and
espresso.

#butfirsthope

We live in a
world that is
full of
devastation and
evil and
darkness.
We also love in
a world that has
given us light
and espresso and
music.
There will be
funerals.
There will be
tears.
But there will
be weddings and
newborn babies
and hands to
keep us warm.
We have the
power and
potential
within us to
choose which
fires to ignite.
Seek the good
and surrender
the burn.
Don't extinguish
hope.
Not yet.
Not ever.

@thenakedmomma

When I Die

When I die I hope that there will be laughter.

I hope that champagne will be served.

I hope that people wear red.

And I hope when people speak of me that this is what they will say:

She hugged too hard.

She laughed too loud.

She felt too much.

She swore too much.

She talked too much.

She wore heels that were too tall.

She wore skirts that were too short.

She had too many tattoos.

She made too many inappropriate jokes.

She asked too many questions.

She drank too much caffeine.

She drank too much wine.

She made peace with being too much for too many.

She was overdressed.

She was never early.

She couldn't sing but that never stopped her.

She couldn't sew.

She couldn't bake.

She couldn't be contained.

She never had a shortage of people in her kitchen.

She made her own traditions.

She stopped using her voice for apologies unearned.

She loved with reckless abandon.

She tried to see the whole world.

She tried to save the corners that she could.

She tried to give her children deep roots and wide wings.

She fell.

She rose.

She danced.

She unraveled.

She let go.

She evolved.

She carried herself as though she was made of feathers.

She never smoothed her wild edges.

She never stopped writing new chapters.

She never stopped chasing the light.

She was a tangled mess.

She was strong.

She was fierce.

She was brave.

She was a badass.

She dreamed out loud.

Her friends were her soulmates.

The ocean was her therapy.

Grace was her religion.

Imperfection was her backbone.

Forgiveness was her freedom.

She lived like there was magic enveloped in the every day.

She lived like there would never be enough time.

She lived like there was fire in her veins.

She lived.

SUMMER

Why I Wear a Bikini

I am 37 years old. I have given birth to four children. And I wear a bikini.

My body is not perfect. But it is mine. It tells stories of a lifetime. The birthmarks, the bumps, the bruises. The testaments of a clumsy but full life. The stretchmarks from adolescence that have never completely faded. The tattoo on the small of my back from a 19-year old's spring break completed at a flea market in Mexico (sorry Mom). The tan lines of wedding bands rarely taken off. The chipped toenail polish of feet that yearn for a pedicure. The calloused fingers from writing too much (though most days it feels like not enough). The map of veins in legs that seem to grow brighter, more present with each year. The hips that are full, the breasts after years of breastfeeding that somehow are not and the abs that will never be 22 again.

I have a body that says life has grown within it. I will not hide it, miracle machine that it is. I will nourish it, protect it and celebrate it. After all, it does house my soul.

And those lives that have flourished within it and now outside of it, are looking at me. *Up* at me. They watch and listen to how I treat my body and soul. They learn how to treat their own. There is great power in the potential of these everyday moments. Our children take in more than we could ever give them credit for.

So before we judge the best and worst bodies on the beach, let's remember that it takes more confidence to be in the sand than it does to stay inside of a hotel room. Our bodies whisper our deepest memories so let's listen to one another with open minds and respectful eyes. And when you find yourself yearning for that 22 year old stomach, remember the wisdom that you have gained with each passing year and that is a breathtakingly beautiful thing.

Rock that bathing suit baby. It is just the gift wrap of your radiant soul.

Two and a half. Just in case you were wondering about the number of errands you can run with four kids and still keep your sanity.

#seeyouinseptembertarget

I Was the Best Mom Before I Had Four Kids

Before I ever gave birth I was the most amazing mother. Just the greatest really. You could have bottled me with a hand stamped, recycled label that would have read "Zen momma". While I still hold on to oh so many of those pre-conception hopes and dreams (most of them have to do with sleep), my fragrance is now combined with an even more overpowering one that I like to call *reality*.

It is human nature to think about the type of mother we aspire to be or perhaps, even more prominently the type of mother we *do not* want to be. Of course my children will be born without the help of drugs (I had an epidural every single time). No sugar, no thank you (I once watched my kids lick a jar of spilled sprinkles off the floor while thinking "one less snack that I have to prepare"). Cloth diapers seem like a very smart choice (um, laundry is my nemesis, pampers became my bffs). Of course, my children will be by my side at all times (where the f--- are my twins?!). I will be on time for everything (I always knew that would never really happen. It just sounds so good).

For a while there it really did feel like we were floating in a Johnson & Johnson's commercial. I gave birth to Lucy at 24 years old and she was the sweetest thing I have ever laid eyes on. She immediately took to breastfeeding then to organic homemade baby food. She loved being carried like a kangaroo in any carrier I put her in for walks or shopping or lattes or baby and me yoga. She was and I hope will always be my saving grace.

It was a no-brainer to have a second. In between my first and second, I suffered a miscarriage which is one of the deepest things I have ever had to grieve. Even though everyone knows someone who has had at least one miscarriage, it does not stop it from being an isolating loss. I felt like I had sadness in my veins. The thing is, the pregnancy gods are always there to make sure we always keep everything in perspective and never get too comfortable with wherever we are in life.

When I was ready, full of hope and peace once more, I became pregnant with Niko before I could even blink. I went through an intensive yoga training with him inside me and graduated from the program two weeks before my due date, secretly hoping I would go in labor with all of those inspiring yoga teachers that could remind me how to breathe. Alas, he was late but he was still destined to be Zen. His birth was exactly what I imagined a birth should be- a stunning miracle. He was born happy and his six year old self hasn't stopped making us happy since.

And then came the twins. Remember that those pregnancy gods attempt to always be fair. Sometimes people have a challenging conception or pregnancy but then are rewarded with an easy labor. Or the challenge can come with toddlerhood (I am sure that it typically always does) or even school age with bullying or anxiety but then you can have less insane teenagers. And sometimes people have special needs children or sometimes go through such unimaginable loss to which I am not going to get into except to say that sometimes God chooses certain parents to be angels on this Earth and sometimes He (or She) wants his angels in heaven early. Thank you to the angels among us, you heal and bring such light.

So we knew we wanted to have more children, we just weren't expecting two at the same time. From the moment they were conceived those two have been destined to be wild. It was actually a relief to find out two were sprouting in there because my pregnancy symptoms felt like they were quadrupled. During that first exhausting trimester, I could have curled up in a parking lot and fallen asleep. I don't mean in a cushy car, I mean directly on the pavement. The slight smell of anything (chicken, flowers, perfume) made me want to throw up my saltine crackers. Then later in my second trimester came full bed-rest because I was at risk for pre-term labor. I told the midwife, "No thank you. I really need walks and prenatal yoga for my sanity and you see I have these other two toddlers to take care of." Midwife: "No. You need people to help you. You are only allowed to get up to go from the bed to the couch if you want to have healthy babies. This is not a request." After I shed a fountain of tears, Steve and I enlisted the help of people that we are so lucky to have. My dear best friend, my sister, flew in from Texas with her family to play with my family. Friends brought me snacks and celebrity magazines. My generous mom and mother-in-law rearranged their work schedules so that every waking shift was covered so that Lucy and Niko could have the best summer and I could follow my bed to couch regimen. It was extremely difficult to be a mom from the couch but I am so grateful that without hesitation or complaint that those beautiful beings were there for us.

At 37 and a half weeks, I was roughly the size of a beached whale, had daily soul on fire heartburn and no longer held the lung capacity left to breathe. It was time. I was supposed to be induced but kept getting bumped so Steve and I walked the mall to enjoy our last moments of freedom while we waited for the doctor's phone call for when we could head to the hospital. Correction: he walked, I waddled. We had to stop about every 10 feet so that I could pee (did I mention I no longer had any bladder capacity either? Those babies took up every centimeter of real estate from my throat to my knees). With my stretched out maternity shirt that didn't quite reach my maternity capris with beads of sweat running down my pale cheeks on this crowded mall August day, I might as well have been handing condoms out to teenagers along the way. Those teenagers were looking at me with genuine fear in their eyes. That is what happens when you get knocked up? Yes, my dear ones. This could be your future. You are welcome, mothers of teens.

This could be your future.

All things considered, their labor was fast (thank you pregnancy gods). I arrived at the hospital at 4 centimeters and went ahead with the epidural so I could dilate and we could both seize this last opportunity in years to sleep. The last time my twins had agreed on anything was to both be head down so I was fortunate to be able to have a vaginal delivery. Three pushes in a few minutes and Sophia was born with a full head of hair and all features radiant. I held her while it was Micah's turn at birth. I didn't realize until afterward that I really had been in labor with her. Micah wasn't quite so ready to enter the world. I had no idea that the cord was wrapped a few times around his neck and his heartbeat was dropping rapidly. Steve told me later that they used forceps to get him out even though he was a pound lighter than Sophia; the doctor had to be faster than what nature could do. The nurses had to pound on his small back to get him to breathe and they asked my husband not to take pictures. I couldn't hear any of the stress of that moment. I just remember not hearing him cry.

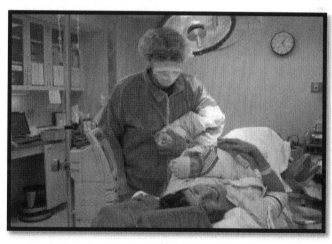

But he was okay. He was a born fighter and she was born to be ten minutes older and full of fire. Together, there is nothing that they can go after and accomplish (or destroy... whichever). I admire their tenacity.

After NICU visits and extreme jaundice that had us first in the pediatric hospital with Micah and then Sophia and a whirlwind of tandem breastfeeding and minutes of sleep a night, we came home. Life felt like a tornado except that I could never reach the eye of the storm. The calm always felt unattainable. I knew we would get there but knew a lot of survival had to happen in between.

There are two things that got me through those (long) days:
1. Try to laugh before crying.
2. Fake it until you can own it.

That is what I know for sure. When you are (strongly) outnumbered, covered in baby food, unsure of the last time you brushed your teeth while someone is painting the white carpet with red nail polish, it helps to be wearing cute shoes. Wine with girlfriends is ridiculously important too.

My twins (now 3 years) still challenge me on a ~~daily~~ hourly basis but at least they can now dress themselves. Just this week, Micah spray painted our kitchen chairs a smurf-colored blue and Sophia poured a bottle of super glue all over her sister's desk (which led to her having random glue polka dots all over her hair and body... awesome). If I can keep them from burning down our home, I know that they have the potential to do great things. There is awe-inspiring strength and glory and bliss within them. They are exactly who I was meant to have. And I will never be bored.

It will, in fact, work against you to have it all figured out before you are a parent. All you really need to approach it is to have an open mind. One of the greatest things that my children have taught me is that life has other plans. Roll with it, baby. And try not to judge the mom at the store with the four wild kids looking like she needs a drink and a prayer.

She most likely needs both…

"My heart is bigger
than my whole body."

-Sophia, age 5

Life with Twins

Here are snapshots of a life with twins. Here are just some of the priceless moments of our last 5 years with these babes in our world. And of course what we have learned...

Most importantly, don't forget to take pictures.

Cheers...

There's a lot of cuteness.

There's a lot of trying to be like Pinterest. Until you realize every project will result in tears.

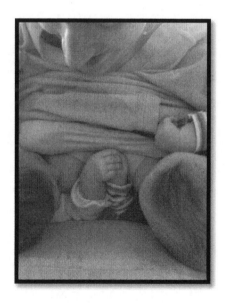

There's a lot of this.

And this. Sharing germs is our favorite.

So is stealing electronics.

Life is a little bit messy.

Or a lot.

Don't worry Mom. We can find the jar of Aquaphor on our own.

They're willing to try anything.
Thanks Uncles.

They will consume things that are not even close to being food.

Seriously...who keeps putting these diapers on?

Duct tape = survival.

When you blink they will do this...

The only time they prefer to wear clothing is actually the places
where they're not supposed to.

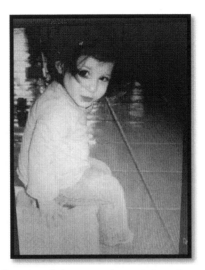

Potty training may have taken 3 years.

Dirt and nudity will find them wherever they go.

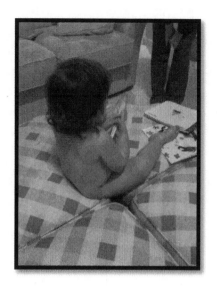

Is there really a better way to read?

Life is really all about the shoes.

And sometimes we are upset because we tried to put on too many pairs of underwear.

Everything becomes a toy. Or a way to get onto a counter.

Or sometimes things are just in their way. Like all of these clothes that were in drawers.

Make-up is the most fun. Especially on Christmas. When we are hosting it.
And momma hasn't put any on yet.

They will find a way to do anything.

And anything can become a swing.

Or a new chair. Like this sink.

Chairs are so much more fun if you don't wear pants.

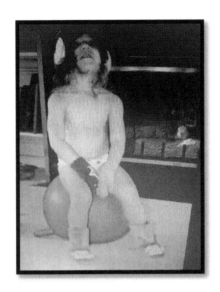

Pants are so overrated.

They can do anything at all.

And everything at once.

They will find a way to get bruises and you will have no idea
what they did.

They literally exhaust themselves to the point of this.

They will find a way to escape. Always.

They will find a way.

And find the keys to the ATV.
Naked.

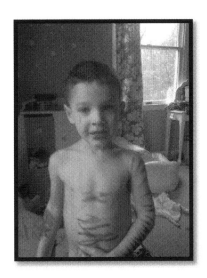

And just when you think they will color on paper...

I swear that we own clothes.

Seriously it is that exhausting to keep up with your twin.

And then the next time you blink, here they are. Clothed and
holding hands.
And you don't know how you all made it.
But you did.
And you try not to do anymore blinking because this journey is
just the most fun.
And exhausting.
And you wouldn't want it any other way.

The Rules of Summer:

Dearest Children,

Hello loves of my life, anchors of my world, angels among us. I love you and I am so proud of you. Can you even believe that summer is here again? Can you even believe that there were ZERO snow days this year so therefore you are getting out a week earlier than any of us planned for? I know I can't. At all. I don't know what I would even do with a bonus week with you all in school. No idea. I mean maybe one or two ideas.
But this is going to be a great summer. And how about the fact that you all don't even go back for the first time ever, until after Labor Day?! THIS WILL BE THE LONGEST SUMMER WE HAVE EVER HAD. EVER. I can't even believe it. Really. I can't. It is going to be great. Absolutely. Great.
But here's the thing: there needs to be a few ground rules so we (okay me) keep our sanity. You are older now, and I know that you can do this. If you follow these rules, I promise you that we will have an amazing summer. That's it. Just a few small rules for peace, sanity and joy.

1. **Chores Before Technology.** If you ever want to see your precious iPods again, make sure your room is clean and your daily chores are checked off. Get them done, son(s). And daughters, you too. I'm checking the closets too. I was a kid once. I'm onto you. The difference is we only had three channels and one Commodore 64. I know you don't know what that is — Google it (something else we lived without, and I don't really even know how).

2. **Be Kind.** You fight, you lose that technology. Work it out. On your own. Kids getting along = happy momma = trips to get ice cream. See, math is useful.

3. **Be Grateful.** If you don't say thank you for the soft serve, you will no longer receive the soft serve. And believe it or not, vacations are not free. So fun? Yes.

Cost saving? No. Manners are free and unfortunately vastly underused. Please dear cherubs, be appreciative.

4. **Wet Towels Do Not Go on the Floor.** On what planet would this seem like a good idea? Your floor is not the place for a mold inducing science project. You have two options here. One: hang up the towel (there are hooks everywhere now because of last summer's constant wetness). Two: wash it. Oh, you don't know how? Don't worry, you are going to take a summer camp week after week called laundry, cooking, gardening, giving back, etiquette and being a good human 101. And I'm your teacher. Welcome to class, kids.

5. **Clean Up After Yourself.** Read it again. And again. You make a mess or pull something out or make a snack or leave your dirty socks in the hallway? Clean it up. Read it again.

6. **Close the Door.** I love you so much. I really do. But if I have to tell you to close the outside door every five seconds this summer, the next time you have ice cream will be when you graduate high school. I do not desire 117 bugs to go into our house or to watch the dollars that are dedicated to cooling it, fly out of that open door. You are so amazing and self-sufficient but this makes me question your future survival in the world if you cannot remember to do this one simple task. Xoxo.

7. **Take Your Slime Making and Your Fidget Spinning and Your Water Bottle Flipping OUTSIDE.** I'm going to bust a blood vessel in my right eyeball if I open the refrigerator door one more time and find my palm stuck to neon green slime. That funky gel is only to be made outside and played with outside and cleaned up outside. If it's raining, you can wait for the sun to come another day. It will, I promise. But my eyeballs and the blood that runs to them, need to stay intact. And the sound of the fidgeting and the constant flip of the water

bottles. I just can't. Eyeballs twitching. I love you. Go flipping outside, out of ear shot please. And close the door.

8. **If You Are Old Enough to Need/Want/Desire to Wear Swim Goggles, You are Old Enough to Adjust Them Yourself.** I believe in you. I do. You do not need me to do this for you. Please be a problem solver. And back when I was a kid, you swam without goggles in all of the chlorine until the whites of your eyes turned the color of heirloom tomatoes. Just kidding. THERE WERE NO HEIRLOOM TOMATOES. There were just plain normal tomatoes. Not that we had those. Our eyes turned the same color as generic pasta sauce in a can, okay? That was the shade of red we knew. And you didn't complain about it. You stayed in that chlorine until your skin was purple and you were almost blind in one eye because you didn't know when you would get the opportunity to swim in a pool again. You are so lucky. You don't even know.

9. **Do Not Even One Time Say That You are Bored.** Not one time. You all know that this word is banned in our house. To me it is worse than any swear word. How can you even possibly be bored? You have a pool, a yard, friends, each other, a computer, a boatload of books and games and I've stepped on twelve of your Legos just this morning (please read No. 5 again). We are literally walking through your toys to get to the outside world. It is not my job to entertain you. It is not. I would be doing you a gigantic disservice if it was. You see, kids that grow up quick to be bored and quick to instantly have the need for someone else to entertain them, can grow up to be adults who need the same thing. And being bored is not an attractive quality to bring to this life. You are more than that. This is a beautiful land we live in and what a glorious thing to have a free summer afternoon to explore. Embrace it. Create. Invent. Paint. Write. Read. Play. Dream. Cleaning is of course welcome too. This is

the secret to happiness — find the magic in the mundane and you will never be bored. Keep seeking magic. Keep feeding your mind. You will never ever regret that.

10. **Have Fun.** Childhood is fleeting. Summer flies too fast. Let's enjoy it while it is here, loves.

Here's to summer.
It really will be a great one.
xoxo

I remember as a kid there being
only two things on my to do list:
1. Play outside all day.
2. Come home when mom rings the
dinner bell (you could hear it from
anywhere in our
neighborhood. Note to self: invest
in insanely loud dinner bell).

That was it. No responsibilities.
Just joy. Sunshine. Sandcastles.
Sprinklers. Fireflies.

And dance with your sister in
completely rad outfits.

#then

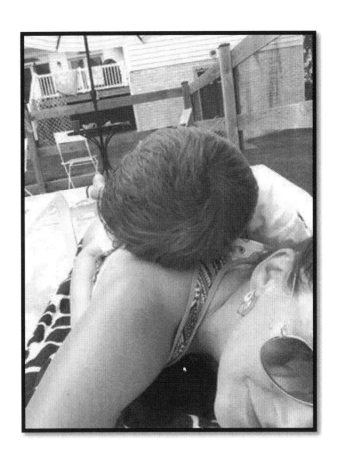

My human blanket.

#whensweatandjoycombine

#now

#illtakeit

My Kids are Hoarders

I'm not proud of my life at this moment.

The thing with hoarding is that you think you will realize it when it happens to you. Or your kids. That your life will be all like, "Whoa there sister. You've got a problem." But the catch is that it's this weird gradual buildup of RANDOM SHIT and you don't really have an "oh sweet baby there is so much ridiculousness taking over your room" until you there is some strange crazy odor that you don't even know what it is or where it is coming from. That is when you realize you're raising a hoarder. And it will frighten the hell out of you. Especially when you realize you really only have two options:

1. Burn the house down.
2. Clean out EVERYTHING.

Option 1 seems like the favorable one I know. But the aftermath of that clean-up seems like even more work than the pain of number 2 so I guess that is the option I am currently procrastinating.

Last night began operation clear out/hoarder no more/maybe one soon day my kids will have floors with a path by cleaning out under the girls bunk beds which is unfortunate because it hadn't been done, well... ever and it is also a bummer because it was going to be one of the "fun" summer projects that I had planned. Okay it was the only summer project I had planned. Looks like cleaning the floors with a toothbrush just entered the itinerary! Happy June kids.

Forgive me, I just need to vent. And procrastinate. If you don't hear from me in a few days, I may actually be buried alive. Please swing by, preferably in a hazmat suit. With a professional carpet cleaner. Most preferably with some Chinese takeout.

May clean inspiration be with us all...

If you're in the mood to
declutter for hours to
have your house look
worse than when you
started, I highly
recommend having kids.

#parenthood #greattimes

The Power of the Poppas

Almost every time I ask my three year old son what his favorite part of his day was he innocently says, "When Daddy came home."

As much time and energy I invest in my children, the relationship I have with them could never be the same as the one that they have with their father. And that is okay by me. I understand. I'm a daddy's girl too. He delivers the play and the fun and the laughter and can do it in these short amazing windows of time. I may give them the quantity but he sure can bring out the quality.

The power of the poppas is a fascinating thing. Our mothers, generous and stunning as they are, have their to-do lists in hand, endless places to be at the same time and they have to keep their (comfortable) shoes planted on the ground. They are reliable. They are constant. It is usually a given that they will always be your number one fan. So safe and nurturing. But the fathers... the fathers get the pedestal. They are the protectors and superheroes of our world. The comedians, the magicians, the fixers of anything that is broken. They have the ability to be stronger than they could ever hope to be when they are looked at through their children's eyes. While we look *into* our mothers, we look *up* to our fathers.

This is my advice for all of you dads out there: own it. Own that red cape as much as you can for as long as you can. When your children are young you are their hero. The only person that can change that is you.

Take your son to gymnastics. Have a catch with your daughter. Hold your newborn baby. Let them dance on your toes. Teach them something that is hilarious. Teach them that there is power in your words. Show them that chores shouldn't default to one gender over the other. Tell them that you are proud of them. Be there. Take them out for ice cream. Take your wife out for wine. Love her and that love will translate to your children. They will learn love, respect and compassion through the way that you treat her. They are watching more than you think that they are so you might as well do them proud.

And to all the men out there who are doing just that and are present for their children: thank you. You are making this world a greater place. Thank you doesn't even begin to cover it.

In gratitude, love & hope...

He went to school to be a priest. She went to school to be a nun. And then they met. It's probably the only time in life that they have ever quit anything. I can speak for my two brothers, my sister and I and our 12 children to say how thankful we are that they did.

Love you Mom and Dad.

What if...

What if you never learned to ride a bike because you were too afraid to fall...
What if you never saw the world because you were too afraid to fly...
What if you stayed with someone who leaked the life out of you because you were too afraid to be alone...
What if you never wrote the story that you were meant to write because you were too afraid of rejection...
What if you never splashed in crystal blue water because you were too afraid of the way your thighs looked in a bathing suit...
What if you dreamed crazy big dreams but were too afraid to go after them...
What if you never reached half of your potential because you were too afraid to grow...
What if you were consumed with so much fear that you forgot to be alive?

Life feels safer when you are sitting on your couch. Life feels scarier when you are dancing on a stage.
But the thing is... only one of those things makes for a great story.

I can hear your excuses: you don't have enough time/money/security, your cat is sick, you have too many children, you're married, you're single, you're tired, you're too old, you're too young...
Let me ask you this: do you have a pulse? Yes? Then don't let your life be swallowed by excuses and regret. They may give you something to complain about but they don't make the beautiful life that you deserve. Make a plan and do all that you can to inch yourself toward wakefulness.
Every. Single. Day.

Until you are six feet under you owe it to yourself to live your best life above ground.
Let's stop losing our lives to fear and letting the what ifs win.
The time to be alive is now. *Right now.*

Let's make it count.

If I just had about 10 more
hours in a day, I would
totally be golden.

#fathertimehelpasisterout

Dear Estella,

Welcome to the world little beauty. You are my sister's third baby girl which makes me one wonderfully grateful aunt. I need to make a few promises to you right out of the gate on this day that you were born. Here is the thing with promises, they are not meant to be broken. I will do everything I can to be a constant in your life, a reminder that I see you, your potential and I will be here.

I promise to love you like one of my own children. Actually, I promise to love you differently than my own children; in a way that makes me appear cooler, hipper than my own children could possibly ever see me. The thing with them is that I have to keep on being their mother. *Always.* Oh so responsible for how they turn out and all the pressure and to do lists that comes with that. But for you and your sisters my responsibility is just to be fun. *Sweet beautiful bliss.* I'll take it.

I promise to buy you adorable, completely non-practical clothing. Of course you need baby skinny jeans. I recently stared way too long at a 0-3 month size trench coat for you that cost twice as much as mine (we will wait for that to go on sale, love). I promise to give you cookies the size of your head and gigantic banana splits. I promise that there will be slumber parties in your future where bedtimes will be ignored. I promise that you will see the ocean. And catch fireflies. And play hide and seek. I promise to laugh with you. I promise to dance with you. I promise to listen to you without judgement. I promise that I will want to hurt the first person that breaks your heart. But I won't. Aunts are not here to embarrass. That's why parents exist.

You are the twelfth grandchild for your Grandma and Grandpa. Lucky number 12. It seemed that for a while there that it would be eleven kids to carry on this great shrieking family laugh of ours but you and your parents had other plans. This speaks to your momma's great strength. She would have jumped through flames to make sure you arrived. She knew her world would not be complete without you in it. She was destined for the miracle that is you. You have made this world more whole.

Every life is a gift. A glorious one that should not be taken for granted. I cannot wait to see what you will do with it. I promise to love you. Always have. Always will.

Cheers to you gorgeous...
Aunt Katie

My kids love when I make them pose next to each other.
Said no mother ever.

#ifyoucouldseetheirfaces

An Open Letter to my Thighs

Dearest Thighs,

You have been with me now, literally, forever. You've witnessed and been one with me through thicker and thinner days. You've been there through the crashes and the cascades. You know what it feels like to reach for the clouds on the springtime swings of childhood. You know what it feels like to have the warmth of a July sun and soft powder sand cradle you at the same time. You know what it feels like to help carry the weight of bringing a baby into the world. You know all about being weightless for a moment in the depths of cool oceans and being so whole and heavy in the all-encompassing place of motherhood.

So I feel saddened and shameful to admit that when I look at you, admiration is not an emotion that I adopt. You are what my eyes first see in a dressing room mirror. Fluorescent lights seem to showcase every line, every imperfection, every dimple of years that are mapped across your edges. When I see you now, it is hard to remember the girl that you used to pedal on a bicycle faster than fireworks on summer afternoons. When I see you now, it is hard to remember that I once saw you as beautiful. When I see you now, I long for an eraser instead of a highlighter. When I see you now, I see the things that are wrong instead of the things that are right.

Which is why I have decided to call a truce.

I am no longer going to complain about you. I am no longer wasting dear moments producing hostility toward you or me for the way that I carry you. I am no longer letting you dictate whether or not we will spend summer in a body length cover-up or in a show you off sweet bikini. I am flaunting you. Because you are powerful and strong, regardless of size. And life is glorious. And the more complaining we do about the way we are built, the more that glory seems to diminish.

Our time is too valuable to pick apart the width of our bodies instead of embracing the pieces that make up the width of our days. Whether it is thighs, or stomachs or breasts or arms or faded images of the way we used to see ourselves. The way I see it, we have two choices: to either let go of our complaints or to do something to make a change. We can go to the gym, or go to yoga or go to a plastic surgeon or buy the spanx. Or do none of that. There should be no shame either way. We have a choice in the way we see and treat ourselves and how we see and treat one another. So let's keep on going and live a life that is lighter and freer because we won't have our negativity weighing us down. We get this one shot at life and our bodies are there for the whole stunning ride.

So thighs, bring it on. You are with me in the drivers seat and the time to press the gas is now.

Let's do this…

To My Children Before You Go Back to School

There are only a few bittersweet days of summer left. A few more sun soaked moments in time before you are carried away to school all day. Education is a vital part of childhood and I never want you to take it for granted. But another vital part of childhood is the carefree summer afternoon. And part of what makes those August afternoons so beautiful is that they come with an expiration date. So my dear loves, enjoy them in all their fleeting glory.
Here is what I want for you before you go to school:

I want to see summer through your eyes.
I want you to be a kid.
I want you to roll down green hills.
And sing.
And explore.
And create villages and draw and paint and wonder as only you can.
I want you to get lost in a book.
I want you to get lost in your imagination.
I want to watch you jump in a pool. Or a lake. Or chase waves in the ocean. Or spin sunlight in a sprinkler.
I want to see you mesmerized by water.
I want to see your bare toes set out on an adventure.
I want to see you pedal faster than the wind.
I want to see what you find between the blades of grass.
I want to see what your hands choose to hold.
I want you to laugh with wild abandon.
I want you to try something new. A food, a game, a talent, a story. Just try.
I want you to release yourself of worry.
I want you to only carry the weight of joy. And possibility.
I want you to practice kindness.
I want you to follow what fills your soul.
I want you to know that you can always ask me the hard questions.
I want you to know that I might not always have the answers.
But I am trying.

I want you to know that I will always show up.
I want to watch you grow. But not too fast. You have the rest of
your life to be an adult. Stay in the magical lane of childhood for
as long as you can.
I want you to be you, glorious you.
I want to hold you just a little longer.

Thank you for showing me summer through your eyes. Thank
you for giving me the best education of my life. Thank you for
the tough questions and the tight hugs and the hard moments and
the hope and the grit and the happiness and the days that once
seemed just too long now seem just too fast. Thank you for you.
You are going to thrive this year. We are going to thrive this
year. And if there are slippery moments, my hands are here. We
all fall. The key is the getting back up. We've got this.
Here's to summer. Here's to the teachers. Here's to fall.
Here's to you...

Sophia: "Mom, why do we
go to bed when the sun is
still out?"

Me: "Shhh, you're so tired
that you're seeing
things."

#bedtimeflandersstyle
#justgotobed

29 Reasons You Should Go On a Girls Weekend

Every year, my closest friends from home that I have loved for over twenty years and I escape our daily lives and spend three nights at one of my friend's family homes on the Jersey Shore. It is bliss. Today is Wednesday and I am still basking in the glow of how therapeutic it felt to laugh for hours on end. I think girls getaways should be the required homework of motherhood. You come back with a spirit renewed. And if that isn't reason enough, here is a list of 29 reasons why.

1. You deserve it.

2. You picked slime out of a child's hair this morning.

3. You don't remember the last time you completed a thought.

4. You forget what it feels like to be called anything other than MMMMmmmoooommmmm.

5. The beach is a completely different experience without children. Like they probably shouldn't even be called the same thing. When you are with your girlfriends you maybe should refer to it as "La Playa."

6. Everything is a completely different experience without children. Restaurants, shopping, sleeping uninterrupted… it doesn't matter where you go, it just matters that you go.

7. Lattes. Coffee shops. Brunch.

8. The current scent of your car can best described as "science experience gone wrong."

9. There are still four weeks of summer left.

10. Priceless therapy.

11. The last time you laughed out loud was when you pretended to during a group text. The last time you really laughed was during a Kung Fu Panda movie.

12. You are able to walk in public without having to do a headcount.
13. Slumber parties. Sushi. Sisterhood.
14. The only things you really need to pack are... well... anything you want. YOU ONLY HAVE TO PACK FOR YOU.
15. You catch yourself singing the Doc McStuffins theme song in the shower.
16. You forget how much fun it is to get ready with girlfriends.
17. You only have to clean up after yourself. And you make approximately one gazillion times less of a mess than your children.
18. You don't have to read a children's menu aloud to anyone.
19. Wine.
20. You can read. An actual book. Or an actual magazine. Cover to cover. Like a boss.
21. You can take a nap.
22. You can actually see the steam rising on your food and can eat it while it is still at that temperature.
23. You can have deep chats.
24. You can carry a purse smaller than your head.
25. You can break out a pair of heels. Or a pair of yoga pants. There is no judgement.
26. You can listen. Really listen. To who your tribe is. To who you have become.
27. You have the best friends in the world and your lives are infinitely richer for having each other. A love like that deserves to be celebrated.
28. It is a beautiful thing to have a moment to miss your kids. And to have them miss you.

29. You deserve it.

So go ahead. Talk/text/send a bat signal to your girlfriends. The time is now to reconnect to the person and people that can become buried under the weight of day to day life. It is a beautiful weight but sometimes we all need to take a moment to have it lifted. Let the mom guilt go, you don't need to justify this. You will come back a better mother and human.

And you owe that to your children. You owe it to you.

Cheers.

Who says that
your friends
can't be
your
soulmates?

You are Sexy

This one is for the warrior women in my life who have shown up time after endless time. This one is for every amazing woman who has reached out to me to say that they read something I wrote and said, "I know. Me too. Me too."
This one is for the women who don't feel like they are enough. The ones who are given mediocre compliments like nice and fine. The ones who need to know that nice doesn't even scratch the surface of their depth. The ones who aren't told enough that they are beautiful. The ones who can't see how sexy they already are.
This one is for the women that we aspire to be, the women that we hold close, the women that we are.
This one is for the women.

Dear Beauty,

We need to talk, so please bring it in real close. I know you've had some hard minutes and moments and months and then there was that whole 2016 year that we'd rather not talk about, but I need you to know this: you are so beautiful. And all of that dark and hard that you have survived? It has only made you more. More sexy, more stunning, more gloriously human. You've shed layers over your lifetime that were no longer needed. The lines you carry now show a life well earned. Let's let go of our comparisons to an idealized unachievable level of what Photoshop believes beauty to be and embrace the brave bodies that we were born into and have sculpted through our days.
We need to redefine what is beautiful, what is sexy and not apologize for being either one.
Smart is sexy.
Strong is sexy.
Brave is sexy.
Curves are sexy.
Shedding your armor is sexy.
Vulnerability is sexy.
Scars and imperfections and hours lived with edges and grit are sexy.
The way you dance.
The way you cry.
The way you stand.

The way you unapologetically burst with laughter.
The way your mouth purses when you apply mascara.
The way you whisper and roar.
The way you carry your yes's and your no's.
The way you balance and juggle and swarm and keep on treading.
The way you know when to hold on.
The way you let go even when you don't want to.
The way you know when it's time.
The way you love.
The way your eyes fold when you say goodbye.
The way you hold your pen, the way you read when no one is watching, the way you pull your hair from your face, the way you take your tea.
The way you spend your Sundays.
The way you show up for battles that no one else can see.
The way you don't realize how beautiful you are.
You are a rare, irreplaceable art form in a brisk, wild world.
You are stunning.
You are seen.
You are sexy.
Own it sister.
Sending you all the light.
All the gratitude.
And all the love that you already possess,

Katie

It became no
longer
enough for her
to live
on the surface.
Here's to
knowing people
in the
deep.

Skinned Knees and Wild Hair

Skinned knees and wild hair. If you were a perfume that is what I would name you. The scent would be of the sweetest season of childhood. The perfect blend of suntan lotion, melted ice cream and summer rain. When people would spritz it on their wrists they would feel... free. Free of worry. Free of care. Free of feet touching the ground.

The thing is though, I'm just not sure there would be a bottle large enough to contain you. I hope there never is. You aren't the type that should ever be contained.

There is so much beauty in your freedom. Wild curls always untamed, dirt under bare toes, grass stains on knees that have fallen tirelessly from legs that want to run faster than your feet can catch up. You are a girl that loves the fall as much as the twirl. My favorite part is that you get right back up to do it again. And again. You have earned your grass stains.

I do wish that I could bottle this moment. This place in time of you belly down on a swing with laughing eyes and having nowhere you have to be but the backyard. I know I will blink and you will be boarding the school bus with freshly brushed hair, matching unstained clothes and shoes that don't have glitter on them. You probably won't even want to wear a purple tutu to the grocery store any longer.

I learned how quick little girls grow by watching your older sister. I wanted all of those sensible things too early for her. All of the control. All of the perfectly combed pigtails. All of the time wasted battling over me choosing the coordinated outfits for preschool instead of giving her the freedom that she wanted deserved. I thought everything had to appear so together because I presumed that it was a direct reflection of me. Of who I was as a parent. I was too caught up in what other people thought of me to let her fully express her own thoughts and style. I didn't realize how much more rewarding it is to let kids just be who they are instead of trying to mold them into a smaller, better version of myself.

I learned. And luckily for me, (I hope) it wasn't too late. Because she was four and Niko was two when you and your twin brother came into our world. Something had to give. Anyone who could dress themselves quickly became my favorite people in the house. The more mismatched the outfits were, the happier her and I both felt. Ballerina costumes and anything with zebra leggings were all the rage. Somewhere in a disorganized box, I even have a picture of her wearing a pale pink sundress with the January snow falling high behind her.

In a few too short weeks, she will be boarding the bus in a matching-much-analyzed-perfect-for-the-first-day-of-third-grade outfit. After we kiss her and Niko goodbye, you and Micah will walk back down the hill to our house by my side for one last bittersweet year. I vow to you this: I will soak in this essence of childhood as much as possible while it is still within my grasp. It won't be long now until I have to set you free. But until then I will watch you be my wild child, laughing, swinging and getting up again in an absolutely crazy fun little number. And I will be there absorbing you in, learning more than could ever be contained.

Loves,

I have to thank you for
listening and being there for
all of the hard truths and the
real feels. I have to be honest
with you about one more hard
thing. As I write this, I have
to let you know that my
husband and I are going
through a divorce.

We have been together for
sixteen years, almost half of
our entire lives. This decision
is the most painful of all of
them. But also one of the
healthiest and hopeful at the
same time.

Stephen is neither the villain
nor the hero of our love story
and I am neither the victim nor
the heroine. We danced on the
line between.

We challenged each others
spaces until too many cracks
that were beyond repair broke

us open. It is not with anger
that we have chosen to divide.
It is with grace, compassion
and courage to watch the other
one soar.

We get this one life. That is it.
We will love and parent our
children with all that we have.
We will put their souls first.
Now. Always.

I am the dreamer. He is the
anchor. We are better people for
having met one another and we
are better people for setting
each other free.

Thank you for reading, for
listening, for being part of
the tribe.

Here's to the next chapter...

Dearest Artist,

I see you undercover, hiding under the mask of life and motherhood. I see your creative ways. I see your hope, your vision and the edges of what you thought you would be when you drift off to sleep. I see that you have hands that used to build such big things that now spend endless moments in water: baths, washers, floors, sinks, that you forget what else they have the potential to do. That water can swallow your days whole. That water can make you forget to breathe, forget to paint or write or sing or dance. It can make you forget to dream. For being so consuming, it can leave you so very empty.

But dear artist remember this: you are doing the most important work and the constant spiral of it all can make us lose sight of that. You are shaping miracles every day. You are a creator of hope, a visionary and a keeper and gardener of dreams. So make sure that you still go after your own. There is time enough for all that stirs your soul.

There is time enough for you.

Go create. The world needs you.

All That Is Needed to be a Good Man

In this season of Father's Day and the flurry of ads selling the latest grilling gadgets and high tech tools targeted for you, I thought we should talk about the tools that you actually need. The tools that make a good man. If you aren't already carrying them in your arsenal, now is the time to stock up because not one of these can be bought at a store.

1. **Love.** Stop rolling your eyes. If this was already abundant, I wouldn't have listed it first. I think that this is where too many men fall short. If you love someone, you really should tell them. Do you think that they already know it? They still need to hear it. You need to be able to look at her and tell her why you do. You need to kiss her like she is your salvation. Yes, still. You need to hold her hand and not want to let go. If she is your person, you should do everything in your power to keep her. If you stopped kissing her and holding her hand and calling her beautiful, you need to think about why that is. And you need to bring it back if it is a love that you want to keep. It all starts and ends here.

2. **Listen.** She wants to be heard but are you really listening? I hear from women constantly about how they don't feel listened to in their marriages. They shut down. They become numb. Put your phone down. Look at her. Men often think that women are such complicated creatures but the truth is there are three keys to keeping a woman happy: attention, affection and appreciation. They are free, powerful and all have the potential to make her feel wanted which will make her want you all the more. It is a full circle, my friends.

3. **Longevity.** Relationships are roller coasters. There are moments that are too slow, too fast, too high, too low, filled with twists and sharp turns. There tends to be a bit of a blend of good and bad screaming and sometimes wondering what the hell just happened and how did you get roped into this thing in the first place. But the key is staying on the ride. Buckle up and close your eyes if you have to.

But just stay on. This is true of romantic love, and it is absolutely true of a father's love.

So to you good men that are also fathers, keep showing up. Know that being a dad isn't a ride that you can get on and off when it is convenient for you. You should want and have a need to be on it for the long haul — even when it is less fun, even when it is the most challenging, that is when you are needed the most.

There is much to be learned in your presence and perhaps more in your absence. The absence speaks volumes. You can't be surprised if you stop being invited on the ride if the people you love have learned to navigate it without you.

To all the good men out there, please keep walking the good path. You are seen. To all the men who veer off the path, it is never too late to get back on it. No cape is required. And you, of course, don't have to take advice from me, I am no expert and probably one of the last people that should be qualified to give anyone life or relationship tips. But I love deeply and I watch the world with wide open eyes. And I was married to a really good man. And he is still there, and he is a really good father, and he still makes us laugh, and he still picks up the check. I will never stop seeing his light. He will never stop showing up. And even though it may be less of a norm, we choose to walk in grace, together and apart. I am eternally grateful for this good man and for the life lessons he has taught me.

Happy Father's Day to him and to all the superheroes among us.

Here's to the good men,

may we see them,

may we thank them,

may we raise them.

I Hope They See

This one is for all the mommas out there wondering if they are seen.

It is for their children and all that we hope and work toward in the everyday. All that we carry that we don't always put into words.

My dear mommas, you are seen. And one day, they will see it too.

I hope they see.

I hope they see her.

I hope they see a mother who was there.

I hope they see a mother who was never too busy to hold them a little longer.

I hope they see her deep flaws and tired eyes and that she wears her imperfections with a lip gloss coated smile.

I hope they see that she tried her best. Even when she fell, she rose. Every single day.

I hope they see that she holds them to high expectations and a higher road of character.

I hope they see that they can trust their life's truths and secrets with her.

I hope they see with every no she says is because of love, not in spite of it.

I hope they see a mother that will fight for them.

I hope they see her as a relentless advocate for what is right.

I hope they see how proud she is of them.

I hope they see that she lives with equal parts of grit and grace.

I hope they see that she builds the blocks of their world not of sacrifice but of strength.

I hope they see that she is the carrier of their worries so they don't have to hold that weight.

I hope they see that she did all that she could to give them a childhood. The good, sweet, messy, beautiful, topped with sprinkles type of childhood.

I hope they see this world with open eyes and that their kindness and words and actions make a difference in it.

I hope they see a woman that worked before they woke up and after they went to sleep and was so thankful to be present in the space between.

I hope they see that in the mountain of laundry and the tiptoes on crumb covered floors and the running late and in the yelling and the frenzy and a to-do list that will never be complete, that she thanked God every night for them.

I hope they see that she travelled roads before them and she will travel roads after them but the magnitude of the roads that she has travelled with them will be unparalleled on her highlight reel.

I hope they see that is all worth it.

I hope they see that she stopped waiting for Superman and everything changed the day that she realized that she herself already possessed her own glorious variation of Wonder Woman.

I hope they see that she earned and rocked her own world.

I hope they see that people can always change for the better.

I hope they see that she will never stop dancing in the kitchen.

I hope they see that she will never stop dreaming.

I hope they see that there is no expiration on motherhood.

I hope they see that she will own it as her greatest role.

I hope they see love.

I hope they see hope.

I hope they see light.

I hope they see me.

I hope they see.

Friends, it only seemed fitting that I gave you, the beautiful, patient, possibly tired and absolutely amazing reader a gift for finishing (or at least flipping through with diligence) this recipe.

It is one of my favorites.

Endless cheers to you…

A Mint Summer Night's Cocktail

Several years ago my sister was living in Rome and I went to visit her for what I will call one of the greatest weeks ever of my life. The food. The culture. The wine. Italy has a lot going on with its fabulous self.

We went to this stunning town called Nemi that overlooked this gorgeous lake and you just felt so close to the sun, the moon and paradise. And to top that there is this little cafe that serves this glorious, from the Italian gods and goddesses, prosecco with these tiny perfect strawberries in it called fragolini. Oh my. That moment, that drink, that view, that would be my heaven.

Just thinking about that place makes me want to immediately book an Italian getaway but now I have all of these children. Instead I figured I would try to bring a little Rome to our deck that overlooks our slip and slide. Paradise can be found anywhere right?

Here is my recreation of prosecco & fragolini but I also added mint in it as well because it is currently overtaking our garden (and I think it makes most alcohol all the more delicious- trust me on this). Hope you enjoy wherever your paradise this summer lies. Ciao bellas...

The Players:

- 1 1/2 cups of mint
- 1 cup of sugar
- 1 cup of water
- 2 Bottles of Prosecco (you can find it in the champagne section or even substitute champagne)
- 1 1/2 cups of frozen strawberries, slightly defrosted

The Game:

I've always been slightly afraid of simple syrup- who has the time for that? But then I made it and realized that I do. It is wonderfully easy and adds enough authentic minty sweetness to jazz up any beverage you add it to. In a saucepan bring sugar, water and mint to a boil, stirring until sugar is dissolved. Reduce heat and simmer for two minutes. Pour through a sieve or colander and cool. The best part is that it keeps covered and refrigerated for two weeks. Simple minty love.

Now onto the prosecco. Place the slightly melty (that is a fancy culinary term) strawberries in your blender or Vitamix.

Pour in all of your mint simple syrup and one bottle of prosecco (or as much as will fit into your blender). Puree until smooth.

In a large pitcher or carafe pour in the remaining bottle of prosecco and then stir in the strawberry/prosecco blend. Add mint or additional strawberries to garnish. Raise a glass to paradise.

Acknowledgments

For Stephen, I couldn't have written this without you. I will never stop rooting for you. Thank you for being my great love story.

I have a crazy amount of gratitude for the following gracious souls that have helped me survive the last chapter (and please consider this an advance thank you for helping me get through the next):

For my sister, Juls, my soulmate. Thank you for everything.

For my home tribe, my soul sisters. Nicky, Angelina and Brenda. Thank you for a lifetime of joy and therapy.

For my local tribe, my hornets. Carrie, Rizz, Jen and Kelly. Thank you for pitching the red tent and answering the bat signal call, time and time again.

For my college tribe, my girls. Kara, Meg, Carly, Emily, Jess and Christine. Thank you for inappropriate group texts; I wish I could have brunch with you daily.

For my root and wing tribe, my family. Mom, Dad, Greg, Becky, Steven, Emily, Allie, Juls, Brad, Hannah, Kora, Estella, Tim, Lena, Justin, Bella, John, Ang, Nik, Travis, Luke, Jake, Max, Fidge, Courtney, Charis and Penny. Family is family and I am so grateful that you are mine.

For my friends and extended family far and wide that I feel so connected to in the deep. Thank you for being tight huggers and relentless soul supporters.

For my editor, Andrew McFadyen Ketchum (say that three times fast). Thank you for helping me beyond words.

For my business partner/boss/guardian angel, Jennifer Novak. Thank you for your unwavering belief in me. I look forward to having deep chats with you and Tech Daddy forever and ever.

For the readers. I see you. I adore you. And it will never ever be a slight thing to me to have words that I have written, resonate with someone else. I have endless gratitude for you.

For my children, my entourage. Lucy, Niko, Sophia and Micah. Thank you for your laughter. You make my whole soul so proud. I love you more than tea.

About the Author

Katie Yackley Moore is the founder of www.thenakedmomma.com and is a freelance writer, real estate agent and a yoga instructor that wishes she practiced yoga more. A Roanoke College graduate that adores coffee shops, laughing until it hurts and impromptu dance parties. She has published a journal entitled "Dream a Bigger Dream" and the children's book "You are a Warrior." You can find her on Instagram @katieyackleymoore (sometimes filtered, sometimes not at all) and on Facebook and Twitter @thenakedmommakt and @therealhousesofdavidsonville.

She started her blog when her twins were about 18 months and running naked in opposite directions. Instead of getting baby fever, she got writing fever and it became her therapy when she was greatly outnumbered.

She lives a happy and imperfect life outside of Annapolis with her children.

Photo credit to one of the loveliest humans ever:
Caitlin Pavon of Kindred Art Photography

Made in the USA
Coppell, TX
18 November 2021

65990087R00142